PETER

Doors in the Walls of the World

~

Signs of Transcendence
in the Human Story

IGNATIUS PRESS   SAN FRANCISCO

Composite cover art:

Path through a Misty Forest
iStock.com/Sjoerd van der Wal
Old Door
iStock.com/Samiylenko

Cover design by
Enrique J. Aguilar

© 2018 by Ignatius Press, San Francisco
All rights reserved
ISBN 978-1-62164-228-2
Library of Congress Control Number 2018931254
Printed in the United States of America ∞

DOORS IN THE WALLS
OF THE WORLD

Contents

INTRODUCTION

Three Philosophies of Life

How many possible philosophies of life are there?

Answer #1: In the beginning, there is only one philosophy of life. For all authentic philosophy begins in wonder. All three of the founders of philosophy, Socrates, Plato, and Aristotle, said that philosophy begins in wonder.

But there are three kinds of wonder:

1. Wonder begins in *surprise*. This is wonder in the emotions. We go on to questioning wonder, which is the second kind of wonder, only when something surprises us or strikes us—when the seas of our emotions are troubled by something thrown into them unexpectedly from outside: a stone, an angel, or Moses—something that parts our inner Red Sea, which is our heart. Our "why" (wonder #2, questioning wonder) is provoked by our "wow" (wonder #1, emotional wonder). I do not wonder why another student comes through my classroom door, but I do wonder why a gorilla comes through.

2. This second kind of wonder—questioning—is wonder in the intellect, guided by the will (the "will to truth", which is far from automatic). When we are surprised, we

then wonder about the what and the why of the surprise. We wonder (#2) about the wonder (#1).

3. Wonder is consummated in contemplative awe. This is wonder in the deepest heart. We marvel at the truths we have understood: at the design of a mosquito under a microscope, of the order of the physical universe under the mental microscope of a mathematician, and above all at ourselves, at our good and at our evil, under the moral microscope of conscience and that most dangerous and wonderful of spiritual adventures, absolute honesty.

Philosophy not only begins in wonder (#1), it also proceeds by means of wonder (#2) and ends in wonder (#3).
   This book is about the third kind of wonder.

Answer #2: When you think about it logically, there are two and only two philosophies of life. For either there are or there are not doors in the walls of the world. Either there is Nothing or Something outside Plato's Cave.
   That sounds very abstract and philosophical. Let me make it very concrete.
   Two people are walking down a street together. There is an old stone wall on their left, too high to see over. As they approach an intersection, the sidewalk and the wall curve around to their left. As they approach the curve, the first walker is absolutely certain that when they turn the corner they will *not* see an angel walking through the wall. The second walker is not.
   Which walker are you?
   Which would you like to be?

A wall is a limit. A door in a wall is a way of overcoming that limit, a way out of the place confined by the walls. The walls here symbolize the physical universe. The doors symbolize escapes from that limit, "morenesses", transcendences. The point of this book is that there are many doors through the walls of the world, many Jacob's Ladders through the sky.

The most famous passage in all of philosophy, at the heart of the *Republic*, is Plato's Cave. In this myth ("myth" means "sacred story"), Plato says that we are all born into a little, dark cave. The cave is the mind that sees only appearances and does not question what they are the appearances of. We are prisoners there, and our necks are chained so that we cannot turn them around, and all we see are shadows on the walls in front of us, and we think that is all there is. But there is much more; and the point of philosophy, for Plato, is to unchain our necks so that we can see the "more". The shadows on the walls of the cave are real, but they are only real appearances that are cast by more-real, more-solid things At first we do not see these things because they are behind our backs. And there is still more: these things cast shadows only because there is a fire in the cave that makes the light, but we don't see that, either, because we can't turn our necks around; so we just take the firelight for granted. Finally, there is a road that leads out of the cave into a whole other, larger world outside. But we don't believe it leads any-where, and besides, it's a hard road to travel, being narrow and rocky. But if we do turn our necks around and see that there is more even in the cave (that seeing is what physical science does), we might wonder what is outside the cave (that wondering is what philosophy does) and actually es-cape.

We ourselves are the prisoners, and the walls of the cave are time and space and matter. The things we see in the ma-terial world are real, but they not only *have* shadows (on the cave walls) but also themselves *are* only shadows of some-thing more. They are the epidermis of reality, like the sur-face of the sea, the surf-face. Plato's point is that what we see is relative to what we do not see, as shadows are the shadows *of*, and relative to, something more real, more absolute, than themselves. There are not only more things in heaven and earth than we dream of in our philosophies, but there are more *kinds* of things than we dream of.

In fact, there are more things than just *things*. There are, according to Plato, also essences, the natures of things, such as Justice Itself or Beauty Itself or Humanness Itself. The beauty of a woman's face is relative to Beauty Itself, and not, as we usually think, vice versa. The justice of a righteous act is relative to Justice Itself, and not vice versa. A human is relative to and judged by his humanness, not vice versa. Material things are changeable, and our ideas are fallible. Our ideas of beauty and justice and humanity may be wrong; they are mere subjective ideas, mere opinions in our minds, and they are relative to the objective material realities we see; but the "Platonic Ideas" are not ideas but Ideas, not subjective opinions but objective immaterial realities, the absolutes to which both material things and our ideas are relative. That is why our subjective opinions and material things can match: because they match the same things, the Ideas or Essences or Forms. The same Justice exists both in a just law and in a true idea of the justice of a just law; that is why the idea can be true. Both things and thoughts (ideas) participate in the same Idea.

So there are not just one or even two but three "worlds" or kinds of reality: objective material things, subjective ideas, and absolute, timeless objective Ideas, Truths, Essences, or Forms. (Forms, "whats", not just shapes.) *Material* forms (shapes) are in both space and time. Our subjective ideas are not in space, as material things are, but they are in time; we change our minds as often as we change our clothes. But Platonic Ideas are timeless as well as spaceless. Wisdom consists in knowing them.

Materialism radically disagrees with this. It says these trans-temporal essences are not Ideas but only ideas, in fact, fantasies, fears, and follies, myths, fairy tales, concoctions of our imagination, mere shadows of material things. Plato's philosophy turns this inside out and says that the things we see are the shadows, and these invisible things are the realities that cast them. Materialism says that the most real thing is matter and that matter, in our brains, produces the false idea that there are minds, spirits. Materialism is really the idea that there are no such things as ideas, only atoms. Plato's philosophy says that the most real thing is spirit, or mind, and that matter is a shadow of spirit, not vice versa. We are in a play, and although the ideas in the minds of the actors are shadows or copies of the things and events in the play, the things and events in the play, in turn, are shadows or copies of what is in the mind of the playwright.

Materialism says that life is not really a play at all, but a chaos on which we impose subjective order by inventing a play. In other words, that life is "full of sound and fury, signifying nothing". The meaning of life is nothing; there is merely the meaning of matter.

Answer #3: We have seen that in one sense (Answer #1) there is only one philosophy of life (wonder) and that in another sense (Answer #2) there are two (materialism and spiritualism). We can also say that there are *three* philosophies of life. Let's call them moreness, lessness, and sameness. For either there are more things or fewer things or the same things in heaven and earth (i.e., in objective reality) as the things dreamed of in our philosophies (i.e., in our subjective ideas). We could also call these three philosophies mysticism (there is more), reductionism (there is less), and rationalism (there is the same). No one of the three has ever been proved or disproved to everyone's satisfaction by science, logic, or the events of history. That is why you still meet people who believe all three of them.

The first and truest one is Shakespeare's, which he puts into the mouth of Hamlet when he says to Horatio (who is astonished to have just seen a ghost): "There are more things in heaven and earth, Horatio, than are dreamt of in your philosophy."

Most great writers, poets, artists, and philosophers, and all the saints and sages, have believed this philosophy. All premodern cultures did. All children do, until they are "educated" out of it. (Some never are, like Shakespeare and Plato and Dante and Dostoyevsky.)

The second philosophy is that there are not more but *fewer* things in heaven and earth, that is, in objective reality, than are dreamed of in our philosophies, that is, in our subjective minds and beliefs. That is reductionism, materialism, cynicism, nihilism, relativism, and subjectivism.

The third philosophy is that there is *the same* number of things in heaven and earth as in our philosophies; that, as Hegel put it, "that which is real is rational and that which is rational is real." In other words, we are know-it-alls: what is inside our mind and what is outside match pretty perfectly. To believe that, you have to be either a genius, or very arrogant, or both (like Hegel).

The three philosophies disagree both about the world and about us.

About the world, the first philosophy tells us that the world contains more than we think; the second tells us that it contains less than we think; and the third tell us that it contains no more and no less than we think.

About us, the first philosophy tells us that we are fools because we believe too little; the second tells us that we are fools because we believe too much; and the third tells us that we are not fools but very smart.

Historically, the first philosophy is traditionalism, or premodernism, the third is modernism (rationalism), and the second is postmodernism (irrationalism).

Every culture in history has believed the first philosophy except one: the one in which you are now living, modern Western civilization, which is now deeply divided between the old philosophy (the first, traditionalism) and the two new philosophies (modernism and postmodernism, or rationalism and irrationalism).

The purpose of this book is to turn back the clock on both new philosophies (which are not really new but old and decrepit) and to sing and shout and blow a trumpet to announce the Good News that the old philosophy is alive and young; that there are doors in the pitiless walls of the world; that there is More, not Less, than we think or imagine, or even *can* think or imagine; to invite us to come out of our little wombs and be born again, to come out of Plato's Cave into an amazingly larger world of real glories, dangers, and adventures, real heavens, hells, and purgatories as great as those of Dante; to meet many kinds of "extraterrestrials".

These are not mere myths. Or, if they are myths, then they are myths that are real, myths that are not a flight from reality but a flight *to* reality. Like *The Lord of the Rings*. That is the most basic reason for the power and popularity of that book: its sense of *reality*. When you turn from that book to your apartment, you do not get the sense that you have turned from unreality to reality, but exactly the opposite. That "mythic" world is real, though its details are of course invented fictions. Our culture is unique because it is demythologized. This book calls for a remythologization.

Myths are stories about what is outside the wall: The Absolute Good, Platonic Forms, God, gods, angels, spirits, ghosts, souls, Brahman, Rta, Nirvana, Tao, "the will of

Heaven", The Meaning of It All, *Something* that deserves a capital   letter.

Every culture teaches its members their identity by a story. Our present culture's story is that we have evolved into the smartest people who ever lived because we invented Science, and Science knows more about the stones in the wall than ever before.

What it does not know is whether there are angels that can come through the wall.

There are. There is *osmosis*. The world is a semi-permeable membrane. There are *extraterrestrials* among us: messengers from another world, undocumented aliens that slip under our artificially erected borders, visitors from across the great sea that separates this little island universe (not mere galaxy but universe) from the many larger continents of reality that are invisible to us most of the time.

The difference between the three philosophies is not about science. All three philosophies accept science in its account of the wall. What they differ about is the angels.

We moderns still have myths, but we believe they are only artifices, fictions, like Alice's Wonderland or the land of Oz. They are not part of the real world. When we look at the real world, even when we look up, we no longer look up at "the heavens", we look up at "outer space"—not full-ness, but emptiness. We no longer hear "the music of the spheres"; we hear "the sounds of silence". We no longer live in Middle-Earth, midway between Heaven and Hell; we live on "the third rock from the sun", midway between Venus and Mars. We no longer live in a world that is a cathedral. The medievals did not build their cathedrals as fictions, as escapes from the world, but as accurate pictures of the world! But we live in a stuffy little ranch house with a low ceiling about seven feet high. The difference is not measurable quantitatively, for the difference between seven feet and 13.7 billion light years is only relative, after all, only a matter of degree. The great question is: Is there a different *kind* of reality?

That's the shock of Plato's Cave: outside it there is another *kind* of reality, not just subjective spirit and objective matter but objective spirit. That's the main point. Plato's particularly Platonic version of what is outside the Cave is not the only one, for the Platonic Ideas are not the only things that make up the "more", especially if you interpret them, as most philosophers do, as mere abstract universals, reified concepts.

Before you were born, your mother's womb was the whole of reality to you. (That's why we are arrested by the story of the escape from Plato's Cave: it is our universal autobiography, inscribed in our collective unconscious.) Now that you are born, you can turn around and see your mother as only a small part of a much wider world, a different kind of world, a world that is not just a bigger womb. You were always in that wider world, even when you were in the womb; you just didn't see it. Isn't it possible, in fact, isn't it likely, that this will happen again at death? That you are living even now in a much larger world than the womb of this material universe, but that you will see it only when you die, when you are expelled from this second womb, this big, fat mother that you call the universe? Isn't it possible that nearly all the great saints, sages, seers, prophets, and poets were right, that all the wise men and women were really wise rather than fools?

But that's not scientific! Of course not. How could science prove that what science cannot prove cannot exist? Is *that* logic "scientific"? Isn't it self-contradictory? Can the scientific method detect the nonexistence of things that are not in principle detectable by the scientific method? In fact, can it detect the nonexistence of anything except a logical impossibility, a self-contradiction? Doesn't certainty about a universal negative require omniscience? Don't you have to have knowledge of everywhere to know that there is no X

The difference between these two philosophies is not just a difference about whether there is anything more than ordinary life; it is also a difference about ordinary life itself. One of Sartre's characters (Roquentin, in *Nausea*) complains that he has "never had any *adventures*. Things have happened to me, that's all." If the first of these three philosophies (traditionalism, or mysticism) is true, then life is an incredible adventure. In fact, it might be a cosmic love story. The point of living might be something like falling in love with something like God. That would be such an adventure that it would make even boring things fascinating.

Before Romeo fell in love with Juliet, he probably found ladies' clothing boring; but after falling in love, whatever Juliet is dressed in is fascinating. Suppose Romeo falls in love with a larger Juliet that is the whole world. Suppose the whole world is Juliet. Or suppose that our Juliet is God and that what God is dressed in is other people. (These two suppositions are not identical, but they are closely related.) Suppose we are all essentially rooms for God to fill. A mysterious and interesting God, of course; not Milton's proper, Puritanical moralist, but someone more like Tolkien's wizard Gandalf, inviting us hobbits on a crazy adventure that is simultaneously a war story and a love story. Before she fell in love with Romeo, Juliet probably found men's battles and business nothing but boring buffoonery. But whatever Romeo does is wonderful because Romeo is in them. Now suppose that to Juliet the whole world is Romeo. She has emerged from her cave.

I have called this "moreness" "something like God". Another word for this premodern philosophy is "religion". But religion is a nut inside a shell. The shell looks something like law or politics or moral rules or institutionalized business or philosophy, but the nut is romance. The shell is an organization, but the nut is an organism. It is alive, like a tiger. The point of religion, the point of all the creeds and codes and cults, is something like sex. Transcendent sex, vertical sex. An invitation to an unimaginable, incomprehensible, ineffable, invisible, incommunicable, eternal spiritual orgasm. That is what the "experts" in religion, the saints and mystics, all say.

Why do priests hear more sexual sins in the confessional than any other kind? Why is lust harder to overcome than any other temptation? Because it's *interesting*. Well, suppose the secret of life is something like sex? Suppose it is something that is related to the sex we experience as sex is related to a tickle? Suppose all of life is foreplay for *that*. No lover was ever bored by foreplay. That's why the medievals built cathedrals.

Do you want to be out of your mind or inside your mind? Crazy or conventional? Creative or comfortable? Nuts or nice? Passionate or proper? Do you want to live for ecstasy or for equality? Do you want blood in your veins or water?

Do you have shining eyes? If you believed the philosophy of this book and of your remote ancestors, you would. You would have the eyes and the heart of a child. It is often said that we live in a youth culture. It's a lie. We live in an old culture. We idolize youth because we are old. We are tired and bored. Ancient cultures respected the old because those cultures were young. They were not bored. (The very word "boredom" is a modern word!) When Arabs, Africans, Russians, or Greeks come to America, they are stunned by how *nice* we are, how polite and passionless and boring. Like old fogies. They think: "Where's the beef? Where's the passion? Are the terrorists and drug addicts the only ones who have any? Why are you more fascinated by your villains than by your heroes?"

How do we become young again? How do we step out of our culture? By stepping out of our world.

We can do that. There are doors.

It's time to turn back the clock, which is the most progressive thing you could possibly do when the clock is keeping bad time because it's slowed by old dust.

We must begin with discontent and with a refusal of reductionism, which is the mistake of both of the other two philosophies. The formula for this reductionist philosophy is "nothing but". It's nothing-buttery. Love is nothing but lust. Minds are nothing but brains, and brains are nothing but soft computers. Souls are nothing but psyches. Heaven is nothing but dreams. Justice is nothing but negotiated power. Man is nothing but a lucky evolutionary accident. God is nothing but a projection. And the whole universe is nothing but a very large quantity of material energy, or perhaps, in the last analysis, nothing but a very, very complex mathematical equation.

To eat real bread with our butter, we must begin by refusing this nothing-buttery. Instead, we must embrace Moreness (which is simply what "transcendence" means). Reality is far, far more than we can see or think or imagine. This is true even in science: most matter is "dark matter"; most energy is invisible; and the structure of everything is radically different from what appears to our eyes and to our imagination. As one great twentieth-century scientist said, the universe is not only greater than we have ever imagined, it is greater than we *can* imagine. If this is true even of the material world, how much more must it be true of Everything?

This book is "escapist". It is about doors in the walls of the world, or the walls of the Cave, through which we can escape our imprisonment. And when you hear people condemn "escapism", ask yourself who hates the concept of "escape" the most? The answer is: jailers.

But this vision is not "escapist" in any negative sense because it does not diminish the world but enlarges it. The world is not evil or illusory. It is real and good, but there is more than the world: that is the good news. Our world is more because it is less, less than all; it is more because it is a reflection of a far greater reality. This is not escapism; it is supernaturalism.

"Natural" and "Supernatural"

This book is about the supernatural, the "transcendent", the more-than-this-world, the stuff outside Plato's Cave. But this is a tricky concept. One source of confusion is that even thinking and willing, which are natural to us, are in another sense supernatural because they transcend the nature of matter. They are not supernatural just because they are invisible, for not everything invisible is supernatural—physical energy is invisible but is not supernatural—and not everything supernatural is invisible, for miracles are supernatural even though they are visible.

You are probably confused by now. Let's try to get these two terms clear, the "natural" and the "supernatural". If you are *not* confused about this, perhaps you should skip this section. It might make you *more* confused.

The life of a human being, body and soul, material and spiritual, visible and invisible, is natural life, life that is natural to us. The word for natural life in Greek is *bios*. *Zōē*, in contrast, means supernatural life, more-than-natural life. Since different kinds of things have different natures, what is natural or supernatural is relative. Life is supernatural to rocks but natural to plants; sensation is supernatural to plants but natural to animals; reason is supernatural to animals but natural to us; God is supernatural to everything else but natural to Himself. He has a nature: He is good, not evil or indifferent; wise, not foolish; living, not dead, etc. This does not make Him finite, because each of His attributes is infinite. But they are positive attributes. He has a nature, a character.

From our human nature *(bios)* come natural thoughts, natural faith, natural hope, and natural charity.

Natural thoughts, like $2 + 2 = 4$, come from our natural human equipment, human reason. Supernatural thoughts, like "God is a Trinity", do not; they come from divine revelation.

From our human nature (*bios*) also comes natural faith, prudential faith (e.g., "Pascal's wager"), but not supernatural faith, saving faith, faith that is a gift of God.

From our *bios* also come natural reasons for the natural faith that consists in believing in the existence of a supernatural Something that is usually called God. Five of the most famous of these natural reasons are Aquinas' "five ways".

But supernatural faith, hope, and charity, which invite God into your soul, are a gift of God and are supernatural not only regarding their object, which is God, but also as to their origin, which is also God: they are not only about God and toward God but also from God. They are gifts, graces.

Natural love, friendship, affection, or compassion, even when it motivates sacrificial and altruistic acts, is from our natural but more-than-biological instincts, and so it is also natural, that is, part of our nature, our *bios*. But charity (*agapē*) is supernatural. No amount of natural affection will produce it. Sartre, quite consistently, denies the existence of this thing (charity), for example, in *No Exit* and in *Nausea*, because he sees that if it existed, it would be supernatural.

This is the distinction between natural and supernatural that is inherent in the New Testament's use of the Greek words *bios* and *zōē*. The terms, remember, are relative: what is natural to us (e.g., language) would be supernatural to animals, and what is natural to animals (e.g., feelings) would be supernatural to plants; and what is natural to plants (growth from within) would be supernatural to inorganic matter. So because *bios* and *zōē* are relative, human souls, though natural in themselves and in relation to anything greater (God, angels, Heaven), are also *supernatural* in relation to anything less, for reason cannot come merely from the material world or organic life or animal instincts. Reason (which in the broad, ancient sense includes moral will [free will] and moral feelings like guilt and joy) transcends the material universe. No amount of complexification of molecules can be the sufficient cause of the reason that knows molecules. No amount of life is the cause of the knowledge of life. No animal instinct knows and judges and chooses which instinct to follow, as a piano player chooses which key to play. The player is not just one of the keys.

Here is another argument for calling human reason relatively supernatural. First Premise: By reason we know truths about the whole universe (e.g., $E = MC^2$). Second Premise: But the knower must transcend the known. The knowledge of a thing cannot be merely one of many parts or aspects of

the thing known. Conclusion: Therefore, reason must transcend the whole universe. Thus we can call reason "supernatural". C. S. Lewis, in his famous argument against natu-
ralism in *Miracles*, uses human reason, not any *divine* miracle,
as his primary evidence for the existence of what he calls
the supernatural. This is true, but confusing, because Lewis
is calling "*natural* reason" supernatural, or miraculous.

To reconcile both legitimate senses of the words "natural" and "supernatural", we need to make a distinction.
Let's call reason and the things that come from reason (e.g.,
deliberate free choice and the appreciation of beauty) "relatively supernatural", and let's call God and the things that
come directly from God "absolutely supernatural". Thus
we speak of human reason as part of our "natural" human
equipment, and we distinguish it, and what it does, from
absolutely supernatural things like miracles, salvation, mystical experiences, and the knowledge of the things about God
that reason cannot discover, fully understand, or prove, for
example, that God loves us or that God became incarnate
in Christ. We know these things only by divine revelation
and our faith in it.

Just as there are both natural and supernatural versions of
faith and love, there are also both natural and supernatural
versions of hope. The hopeful yearning for something more
than we can get or even imagine getting in this world, the
longing the Germans call *Sehnsucht*, is part of our nature,
though its object is supernatural. So that is a natural hope.
But our "yes" to God's revealed promises—our hope in
them—is supernatural, both in its object (God) and in its
subject or origin (God).

This book is about things that are absolutely supernatural,
i.e., supernatural not only in relation to matter but also in relation to human nature. "The walls of the world" in which

we find doors do not merely refer to the material world outside us but also the natural human world within and among us. It is God, the absolutely supernatural, who comes through these doors, though usually anonymously.

I hope this has made things clearer. If not, do not despair; this book will be interesting and profitable even if these two key terms are not as clear as they ought to be.

Books are boats. Come aboard this boat as it allows the currents in the river of reason and inquiry and investigation to carry it around unpredictable curves of the river and into undiscovered countries and, finally, into an immortal Sea.

Life as a Great Story

This book will not be an abstract philosophy of eternal truths and values but a story and a journey, because it is about the meaning of human life, and life is a story and a journey. Story is the most basic of all human arts; all human cultures cultivate the art of storytelling: it is the surest cultural mark of the human.

In *The Lord of the Rings*, Frodo and Sam, trudging across Mordor on their perilous and almost impossible heroic quest to destroy the Ring of Power, put the greatest of all "existential" questions, the formidably abstract-sounding question of the Meaning of Life, into wonderfully concrete terms: "I wonder what kind of a story we're in."

Life is a story. That is obvious to anyone but an academic or an ideologue. But what kind of story? The only way to answer that question about stories is by stories: little stories that are images of or analogies to the Great Story. So here are ten little stories. Some of them are from writers far greater than I; some are my own.

The idea that life is a story implies that there is a Story-teller outside the story. So the story is a Door to More, a More Door instead of a Mordor (to put it in terms of *The Lord of the Rings*).

Every story, whether real or fictional, whether spoken or written or acted, has five dimensions. To be a great story, a story must be great in all five of these dimensions, just as in order to be a morally good act, an act must be right in all three of its dimensions: the act itself, the motive, and the circumstances; and just as in order to be a healthy human body, a body must be healthy in all of its organic systems: the nervous system, the digestive system, the muscular system, the reproductive system, the circulatory system, etc. The five dimensions of every story are:

1. The plot
2. The setting
3. The characters
4. The theme
5. The style

If human life on earth is a story, it too has these five dimensions. And in each of these five we find Moreness, we find Transcendence, we find doors in the walls of the world, pathways out of Plato's Cave, Jacob's ladders to Heaven.

The five most important human enterprises, the five subjects that are the most important to learn, the five things that distinguish us from animals, are

1. History (which is about the plot of our story),
2. Physical Science (which is about the setting),
3. Psychology (which is about the characters),

4. Religion and Philosophy (which are about the theme), and

5. Art (which is about the style).

(By the way, psychology cannot be an exact science or a merely physical science because its objects [we] are neither exact nor merely physical. For that reason, one learns much more psychology from good friends and good novels than from textbooks and from contrived experiments, useful as these may be.)

Each dimension is more than it seems; each is an example of Hamlet's philosophy of life, that "there are more things in heaven and earth than are dreamt of in your philosophy." Each is a window in the hard, pitiless walls of the world. And through each we can see Something More.

They are more than just windows: each is also a door, an anticipation of the great door through which we will all walk at death. Because of these doors, we can begin to live the life of Heaven on earth. In fact, we had damn well better do just that (I choose my words carefully) because if we don't have any Heavenly roots here, how can we be transplanted There?

Here are some travelers' tales of a far country that you have never seen but that is at the end of the road on which you are now traveling. Is this "escapism"? Is it "escapism" to have a windshield as well as a rearview mirror?

I

The Plot: Life as a Story

The plot is not only the most important of the five dimensions of a story, but the very essence of a story. In fact, the story *is* the plot. That is why the first question children ask about the story is "what is it about?" Aristotle, who had the common sense of children, said the same thing: that the plot is the essence, or "formal cause", of the story.

Plots are not abstract schemes. They are concrete particulars. Therefore, to find plot-windows in the walls of our world, that is, signals of transcendence in our story, I begin, not with abstract principles, but with concrete analogies and examples. Here are ten stories that show rather than tell the strange plot of *our* story.

In the plot itself, we find many strong fingerprints of an Author, a brilliant and interesting Author; they are signs of what used to be called Divine Providence and is now often called Intelligent Design. That idea is not hard science (it's not strictly empirical and quantitative), but it is certainly good philosophy.

To read the story, you need more than logic, at least more than mathematical logic. You need intuition and appreciation; you need the art of reading a good story. That means following not just straight lines but crooked ones. For in this surpassingly strange world in which everything is connected in the most unpredictable and apparently random ways, the divine storyteller is telling our human story by writing "straight with crooked lines". The lines of spiritual gravity, like space itself, are not straight but curved. They are like the winding streets of an old city like London rather than the straight streets of a new, modern, planned city like Manhattan. Good stories are not linear. Emily Dickinson said in one of her poems, "Tell all the truth but tell it slant—"

In this strange city, everything is connected and nothing is superfluous. How many acts of good or evil are needed to make a difference, to save or lose your world, or even the whole world? The answer is one: every one of them.

I will try to show this first by a story whose protagonist is a drop of water. The story has no human characters, so it is therefore not properly a story but a parable.

Story #1: The Colorado Water Droplet

When you drive across the country through Colorado, you come to a marker in the Rocky Mountains that says "Continental Divide". Sometimes the marker will explain exactly what this term means. The Continental Divide is the line that divides the continent of North America into two parts, which here are the east slope and the west slope of the Rocky Mountain range. If a drop of water falls from the sky one inch to the east of the Continental Divide, it will continue to fall, or sink, eastward and will eventually find its way to the Atlantic Ocean or to the Gulf of Mexico, which opens into the Atlantic. If that drop of water falls one inch to the west of the Continental Divide, it will end up in the Pacific.

This is literally true and logically necessary. For there must be *some* place where one inch makes the difference between three thousand miles. Although there are a trillion different paths by which each drop can go, there is not one that does not lead eventually to one or the other of these two opposite destinations. Similarly, although there are a trillion paths by which each individual can travel through the world, there is not one that does not eventually lead either to life or to death, blessing or curse, Heaven or Hell. And there is not one act that a person can do that does not contribute to one or the other of those two journeys, one vote that does not make a difference in the Great Election.

The next story shows the same principle in the world of human gravity, not physical gravity; that is, in the world of human love.

Story #2: The Bouncing Acorn and the Bouncing Sperm

Once upon a time, over a hundred years ago, your great grandfather, who was then in his twenties, was sitting on a bench in a park and looking south, to face the noonday sun, when a squirrel dropped an acorn directly behind him. It hit a branch and bounced east rather than west and therefore fell into a pile of dry autumn leaves that was a few feet to the left of where your great grandfather was sitting. It made a sudden crackling sound that got his attention, caused him to look up from the book he was reading, and turned his head in that direction. With that turn of the head, he noticed a girl sitting on another bench some distance away. He thought her very pretty and plucked up the courage to saunter over to her and politely ask her permission to sit on her bench. She smiled yes, and they struck up a conversation. One thing led to another, and she eventually became your great grandmother.

If that squirrel had dropped that acorn one inch more to the west, it would not have hit the branch or bounced into the leaves or made a crackling sound or got your great grandfather's attention, he never would have met or married your great-grandmother, and you would never have existed, and neither would all your children and all their descendants all the way down to the end of time. And all the things that all of them did and will do would never have been done.

If one of twenty million sperm cells had not bounced off its siblings in just the right way to get into the taxi of your mother's ovum before the other 19,999,999, you would not be you.

Bad Lawyer Joke: What's the difference between a lawyer and a sperm? Answer: One out of twenty million sperm becomes a human being.

Story #3: One Grain of Sand

The third story is fictional, but it may well have been fact. For it shows how history does in fact work.

Long ago, two kingdoms were at war. The first kingdom's capital city was defended with impregnable walls. The second kingdom's only hope was a sudden surprise attack during the day when the gates of the impregnable city were open.

As the cavalry of the attackers bore down on the gates, the gatekeepers, caught by surprise, strove to close them. They had to move the great gates over sandy ground, and there had been a sandstorm the previous night, so the bottoms of the gates had to scrape over some sand in order to close. The more sand there was, the slower their movement.

The number of grains of sand on the ground was many millions. How many grains of sand would it take to slow the gates to the point where they did not close and lock before they were hit by the battering rams of the attackers? No one knows that exact number, except perhaps the angels. But there must be such a number, and therefore there must be one grain of sand that, if it were present, would keep the gates open and allow the conquest of that city and the defeat of that kingdom.

Thus one grain of sand can destroy a kingdom. In fact, one grain of sand did change a kingdom, for it changed a dictatorship back into a kingdom. That grain of sand, in Oliver Cromwell's kidney, killed him at the height of his powers and saved England and, perhaps also, in consequence, her colonies in the Americas, from continuing his dictatorship and "protectorate". Pascal wrote: "Cleopatra's nose: if it had been a quarter of an inch longer, the whole history of the world would have been changed."

Story #4: The True Causes of World War III

This next story is only fiction. But it could very well become fact. The time is the near future.

History was coming to a point, as it often had: Thermopylae, the Rubicon, the Milvian Bridge, Lepanto, Trafalgar, Waterloo, Gettysburg, Stalingrad. This time not just one civilization but the whole world poised breathless on the brink between life and death, like a suicide jumper with one foot over the ledge. Nuclear power had proliferated, as all powers had always done. Terrorist regimes threatened sane ones, and each other. Nuclear powers sat glaring at each other across the global table like poker players in an Old West saloon, each convinced the other was lying, each ready to reach for his gun, each afraid both to shoot and not to shoot, each afraid of war and of peace. Earth poised over the abyss as fingers poised over buttons.

Most of the world had lived in comfortable denial and thus pretended to be surprised. But for many years, the seers had seen this rough beast slouching toward Bethlehem to be born. And the world no more knew how to cope with this Antichrist than it had known how to cope with Christ.

Most of its philosophers and scientists had taught the world that free will was an illusion; that abstractions like History and Fate and Necessity and Economics and Genetics moved men and women around like pieces on their chessboards, not vice versa. Mothers who listened to experts who proclaimed themselves "pro-choice" believed they had "no choice" but to kill their unborn children. The good news of free choice was proclaimed only by those who, like Moses, called them to "choose life." But that was too simple for confused and sophisticated adults to understand. They were persuaded that Science had proved Determinism, and so they were in the process of killing the spiritual child of a free conscience and free will in their souls so that they could then kill the physical child in their wombs. But this spiritual child (conscience and free will) was far older than they were and was still alive and was still pointing to the gate of choice, like Baby Jesus in an icon pointing at his Mother. But this gate was closing. At some point, one more grain of sand would close it.

No one (except perhaps the angels) could number those grains of sand or see which grain would be the last. For each grain was an invisible atom in an invisible finger on an invisible button, and the finger was getting heavier and closer to the button. At a certain moment, the invisible forces of life and death were exactly equal, like the raindrop falling on the Continental Divide or the nut falling from the squirrel in the tree or the gate that was poised to close at the last minute. One additional grain of sand would stop the gate from closing.

That was the fundamental fact, as seen by the angels. The names, dates, places, policies, statistics, troops, and weapons were only the surface expressions, visible to human eyes, of the universal forces of life and death. They were the molecules of the muscles of the face that was moved to smile or to frown by the invisible free forces within.

Sarah Hyman lay dying in a nursing home called "Morning Glories". She had been dying for years; indeed, she had been dying for ninety-five years. For she had been born into a world of death. (What kind of a world is that? Imagine a pregnant woman giving birth crouching over a grave.) But this world was not only a world of death but also a "culture of death" and, worst of all, a culture of the denial of death and, therefore, the denial of life. The medievals had prayed, in their litany, "From a sudden and unprovided death, good Lord, deliver us." But what the old world had feared, this brave new world had desired: a sudden and unprovided death, a death in one's sleep rather than awake, a death in the dark rather than in the light. For when life is lived in the dark, death is also lived in the dark.

Sarah was in what the "experts" had called, with an obscenely arrogant insult, "a semi-vegetative state". A few small cinders still smoldered in her inner ashes. Sarah could communicate only by hearing, not speech, and by squeezing your

hand in reply. However, what her two sons, Isaac and Ishmael, saw in that bed was not Sarah but a bag of skin and
bones in "a semi-vegetative state". They had long accepted
into their mind the Trojan horses of rationalization that had
been given to them by the "experts". Because these "experts" had studied twentieth-century history, they did not
carve their Trojan horse out of words like "life unworthy
of life" or "the final solution", since these euphemisms had
already been invented by earlier, similar "experts"; but they
used words like "life with dignity" and "death with dignity", instead—which, like most ideological slogans, really
meant exactly the opposite of what they said.

Nearly everyone had seen individuals die, but no one had
ever seen a whole world die before. The world had as much
difficulty in making real to itself the fact that it could be
dying as Sarah's sons had in making real to themselves the
fact that Sarah was still living. But both worlds, the one
inside Sarah and the one outside her, were equally poised
at the Continental Divide between life and death.

Sarah's life had been extraordinarily ordinary, in her pas-
sions, her pathos, and her pieties. Only to her family and
close friends had she been unique: the most common unique-
ness, the most universal of particularities. She had suffered
the blessing of a long life and had outlived all her siblings
and even her children except Isaac and Ishmael. Her life was
now a psychological "burden" on them and a financial one
on the nursing home and the insurance company that shared
the cost of her maintenance. The head of "Morning Glories", a psychologist named Dr. Cares, had summoned the
two brothers into her office to "reassess" Sarah's "care".

The office looked dignified but relaxed, with pastel colors
and simple furniture. Dr. Cares was a mature, professional-
looking woman who over the years had carefully cultivated

a demeanor to fit her situation; every muscle in her face moved to paint a picture that said both "professional" and "personal", both "competent" and "caring". Her strategy was to suggest to the brothers, but only subtly and indirectly, that Sarah's care was a burden, not to her nursing home, but to them. (Psychologists call this "transference".)

Sarah had caught a bacterial infection, a common cold that was threatening to become pneumonia. Her lungs, like overused shopping bags, could barely receive and discharge their load of breath, their groceries of life. Antibiotics were routinely called for and would probably have cleared up her condition in a few days, followed by a return to the status quo for perhaps many more months or even years. Dr. Cares made the subtle suggestion that Sarah was already in the long-term dying process and that there was a "compassionate" alternative. Her sons were made to feel that their choice was not between life and death but between a mercifully short death and an unmercifully long death. They were also somehow made to feel that the choice had already been made, and not by them or by her. Providing this ordinary care was labeled "prolonging her suffering" even though it would have *mitigated* her suffering. The labels did the work of decision. Reason and will were not invited to this meeting. They were anesthetized.

Still, kinship and ancient instinct protested, and the brothers hesitated. So elusive are the motions of motivation in the layers of psychic silt in the city of the soul that it was very hard for them to distinguish reasons from rationalizations. Such honesty was not impossible, if they had passionately desired it. But they both knew that if they dared to ask the question of "life or death?" they could not "choose death", so they did not dare to ask the question. That would have required passion, like salmon swimming upstream. Like dead fish, they floated comfortably downstream on the quickly running waters of Dr. Cares' rhetoric.

But Sarah was still choosing life, on a level that was visible, not to the outer eye, but only to the inner I. She was offering herself and her sufferings to a vaguely conceived but honestly believed deity. The offering was being made largely by habit rather than free choice, but it was a habit that had been cultivated by many free choices, and therefore her offering was free. Her habit was still bearing fruit, like a dying tree; and that fruit, though untasted by any man on earth, was received into the heavenly stomach that infallibly digests each earthly fact. Like all words on earth, the last word she uttered lived on in its heavenly echo in eternity.

She began the "Sh'ma Yisrael", the prayer that defines every Jew as the "Shahadah" defines every Muslim. Her spirit commanded her lips to speak. They did not speak, but her spirit did. The first word, "Sh'ma", reverberated between her will and God's like an echo between two walls of a canyon. Was she asking the Almighty to hear and echo her will, or was she echoing His command for her to hear His? Precisely because that question was unanswerable, her prayer was real.

Prayer, like life, takes time. Half a prayer is only half a prayer; otherwise, the second half is superfluous. If prayer makes a difference, then every part of a prayer must make a difference, like every grain of sand beneath the gates.

By her sons' choice, she had been denied the medication that would have given her the strength to breathe another breath. So the prayer remained unfinished. The "Sh'ma" remained without its "Yisrael", like Adam without his Eve. The two words remained in two different worlds: the first in the world of actuality, the second in the world of potentiality only. And as the poet had written, "Between the potency and the act falls the shadow." Sarah breathed her last at exactly one second before 11 P.M. Everything finite is divided by time.

To the unblinking, unsleeping eye of the angels, each thing is, quite simply and exactly, itself. They do not understand organisms by observation of their attributes, as biologists do; they deduce the attributes from the essence, as geometricians do. They register each particle of fact, each photon of truth, as part of their finite access to the infinite Mind of God in which every particle of temporal fact is a part of the eternal whole and gets its meaning from its relation to every other part of the complex painting that is history. We know history from its outside and from our place in time; angels know it from inside the Mind of God and from their place in eternity. Spirits have no "outside".

Among these particles of fact, perfectly known, was Sarah's prayer. It was one particle among trillions, but it was, it existed, and whatever exists makes some difference. Such is the law of the universe, both physically and spiritually. There is a spiritual gravity, of which material gravity is the analogy. In the physical world, gravity is a force that connects every particle of matter in the universe to every other. It is precisely measurable by two finite quantities, two variables (the mass of the two particles and the inverse of the distance between them). So it is in the world of spirit: there is a force that connects every spirit to every other spirit by two similar variables, the spiritual mass of the two "particles" (i.e., the persons and their acts) and the spiritual distance or nearness between them (i.e., the relationship between them). "Spiritual mass and inverse distance" is another term for love.

Love is to the spirit what light is to matter. Like physical light, love is both wave and particle, both discontinuous and continuous, both corpuscular and undulatory, both quantitative and qualitative. This single force appears to us as broken into many different forces by time and space, as light is broken into different colors by a prism.

One of the primary colors of this cosmic force, this "love that moves the sun and the other stars", is called prayer. Each prayer is like a grain of sand that is dropped, not into the desert beneath the gates of the earthly city, but into the Mind of God and the Heavenly city, like a pebble dropped into a pool. Every pebble makes ripples there, as every gravitational event makes gravity ripples throughout the universe.

The first pebble was thrown. Its name was "Sh'ma". The second pebble was not. Its name was "Yisrael". It remained in the hand, not given to the pool. Together, the two would have sufficed, like Adam and Eve, to fulfill the divine command to be fruitful and multiply. One alone did not suffice. The Continental Divide lay here. For it must lie somewhere.

The first missiles were launched at precisely 11 P.M. The human finger that fell on the final button quivered a tiny bit, like the drop of water, the sperm, or the acorn. The owner of that finger was not absolutely sure he would be able to press that button when commanded to do so. His heart, too, was poised over a Continental Divide. One more prayer would have sufficed to stop him. But the prayer was not made. And the world was not saved.

There is a Jewish saying made famous by *Schindler's List*: "He who saves one life saves the world." One meaning of that saying is that each individual is a whole world, not just one of many ingredients in the world of objects, but a unique subject in whom the whole world is reflected in a unique and unrepeatable way. So whoever destroys a man destroys the world.

But another meaning of that same saying goes back to the story of Abraham bargaining with God to save Sodom and Gomorrah. There is a legend that in every age God spares the world the destruction it deserves only because there are a certain number of Abrahams, righteous men and women who keep the world alive by their righteousness and their prayers, by the mass and the gravity of their righteousness reverberating on the walls of the divine mercy. No one but God knows who these righteous are or how many there are. The number is variously ranked at ten, twelve, twenty, or forty. God told Abraham that it would have taken only ten righteous men to save Sodom and Gomorrah, but there were only four. Six more saints would have saved two cities.

You may be one of these righteous persons. The life you save, or fail to save, may be the life of the whole world. For to everything in time there is a limit, a number. And no one knows what that number is until it is too late.

If our prayers and our loves make a difference, the point of this legend must be true. For if it is not true, then our prayers and loves do not really make a difference.

Another way to say exactly the same thing as "He who saves one life saves the world" is that "each of us is responsible for all of us." That is the point of Dostoyevsky's great novel *The Brothers Karamazov*, which we will explore a few pages hence.

This is why we must all be neighbors to each other: because we *are* all neighbors to each other. Jesus made the same point much more simply in the parable of the Good Samaritan. Its point is not just ethical: that we *should be* each other's neighbors. Its point is metaphysical: that we all *are* each other's neighbors. The reason we should be each other's neighbors is because we are. In fact, all moral evil consists in being what we are not (sins of commission) or not being what we are (sins of omission). Morality is rooted in metaphysics, and the truest metaphysics is mysticism.

Story #5: The Cheap Egyptian Tailor Who Saved the World

This story, unlike the last two, is fact, not fiction. It takes up more than half of the book of Genesis. Read it yourself, by all means; my summary is thin, quick, and dull.

Joseph was Jacob's favorite son, which provoked his brothers to jealousy. So they sold him into Egypt as a slave. But he was so enterprising that he worked his way up to become the steward, or right-hand man, of the household of Potiphar, the Pharaoh's right-hand man. However, when Potiphar's wife tried to seduce Joseph, and he detached himself from her grasp, his mantle ripped apart in her hand. Angry at Joseph for refusing her advances, she accused him of attacking her; and that ripped mantle was the piece of circumstantial evidence that convicted him and put him in prison.

About that mantle: there were no department stores in ancient Egypt, so clothing was supposed to last a lifetime, not to rip apart in a woman's hands. The cheap tailor who wove that mantle had cheated on the threads. Now see the consequences of that little act of cheating.

In prison, Joseph befriended Pharaoh's butler and baker, who were also out of favor. Both had dreams that they told Joseph, who had the gift of interpretation of dreams and visions. As Joseph predicted when he interpreted their dreams, the butler was restored to favor and the baker put to death. But the butler, when restored to favor, forgot Joseph's plea to remember him to Pharaoh, until Pharaoh had a dream that none of his wise men could interpret, a dream in which seven skinny cows ate seven fat cows. Then the butler remembered Joseph and his gift of interpreting dreams, told Pharaoh about him, and got him out of prison. Joseph not only interpreted the dream but saved the country from starvation. For the seven fat cows symbolized seven years of plenty, which would be followed by seven years of famine (the skinny cows). Following Joseph's advice, Pharaoh stored up extra grain from the seven fat years for the seven lean years, made himself rich, and saved his people from starvation. For this advice, Pharaoh rewarded Joseph by making him second in the kingdom.

Meanwhile, Joseph's family, the only seventy Israelites in the world at the time, were starving back in Palestine and heard that there was plenty of food in Egypt. So Joseph's brothers went to Egypt to buy grain. By disguises and holy trickery, Joseph reconciled with his brothers and inveigled his whole family, including his old father, who had thought him dead, into coming to Egypt to live and survive.

Generations later, the Jews had multiplied, been enslaved, and through Moses and the Exodus were forged together as a people. It was this people that God prepared as His collective prophet to the world and as His landing field when He became incarnate to save the world. God prepared the world for its redemption through the Jews. Without them, no hope.

But there would not be a Jew alive were it not for that chain of events and, therefore, for each link in it, including that cheap Egyptian tailor, and perhaps even for the one weak or missing thread that made the difference between Joseph's mantle ripping and not ripping. Our salvation depended on that tailor, or perhaps on that one thread. God, indeed, writes straight with crooked lines. The crooked lines make up the walls of the world; the straight writing that is seen through them is the divine fingerprint, the More, the door in the wall.

Story #6: Thornton Wilder's Tapestry

Thornton Wilder, in *The Bridge of San Luis Rey*, tells the story of Brother Juniper, a Franciscan priest in Peru, who is losing his faith for the two strongest reasons in the world, according to Saint Thomas Aquinas—that is, for the two objections to the existence of God in the *Summa*. In two words, they are evil and science. If God is all good and all powerful, how can there be evil? And if science can explain everything in our experience without God, what rational need is there for God?

When one day the rope bridge referred to in the book's title breaks and plunges five young people to their untimely deaths, this is Brother Juniper's last straw. He makes a deal with God in prayer. He says he cannot, as a rational man of science, continue to believe in God if He does not provide him with at least some data. He does not demand proofs (that is unfair and unscientific), but he does need at least some clues. Then comes the famous image, which Wilder copied from Jean-Pierre de Caussade's spiritual masterpiece *Abandonment to Divine Providence*, the image of the tapestry. If God is God, He must be the greatest storyteller, and the story of human life on earth must be the most perfect of all stories; but we do not see the front side of the tapestry of that story, for we are on the back side. We can, however, expect to see some loose threads on our side of the tapestry that are clues, that is, signs, pointers, hints, suggestions, rather

than visions or proofs, of the perfection of the picture as
God sees it.

Brother Juniper then spends the next few years of his life
trying to read the loose threads of these five lost lives by in-
terviewing the victims' friends and family members, reading
diaries, and other relevant research. At the end of his search
for data, he confesses to God that He has succeeded. It still
takes a leap of faith to trust God with this crazy story, but
at least there are reasons, there is data: the threads of the
story that we see seem to form a pattern, though only seen
"through a glass, darkly". The concluding image is one of
the most memorable lines in religious literature: "Some say
. . . that to the gods we are like the flies that the boys kill on
a summer's day, and some say, to the contrary, that the very
sparrows do not lose a feather that has not been brushed
away by the finger of God."[1]

Those are the only two possibilities. Divine design is either nothing or everything; and if it is everything, then it
extends even to randomness and apparent meaninglessness,
to the puzzling presence of evil and the absence of scientific
proofs. The hypothesis of faith may not be provable, but it
is believable. The doors in the walls of the world may be
only loose threads, but they are there.

Story #7: Mark Helprin's Perfect Painting

What Wilder does in his image of a tapestry, Mark Helprin
does in his image of a perfect painting, which is kept in the
mansion of one the protagonists of the story. It, too, is a

[1] Thornton Wilder, *The Bridge of San Luis Rey* (1927; New York: Harper
Perennial Classics, 2003), p. 9.

Door to More. In both cases, the "more" is not another thing, like an angel, or another event, like the Incarnation, but another relationship among all things and events: a perfect relationship among imperfect things.

This is the vision behind Helprin's unclassifiable, indescribable, and wonderful novel *Winter's Tale*. (Don't judge the book by the stupid movie that is an inexcusable, dumbed-down travesty of it.) The point of the complex plot is put in the shortest chapter in the book, which I quote below. The point is that the whole of human life, like a painting, is far more than the sum of its parts; that the crazy, complex story that nature and man together have conspired to create all makes sense when viewed, not from the partialities of time *of which* the story is made, but from the fullness of eternity that is what the story *is*, or is made *into*. Like Wilder's tapestry, this image sees life as a masterpiece, even though it seems to be a mess; a cosmos that seems to be a chaos. The individual parts (the characters and events) make little sense if time is everything and everything is time, but they all make perfect sense when seen from the viewpoint of the final, timeless whole. Here is Helprin's version of that vision:

NOTHING IS RANDOM

Nothing is random, nor will anything ever be, whether a long string of perfectly blue days that begin and end in golden dimness, the most seemingly chaotic political acts, the rise of a great city, the crystalline structure of a gem that has never seen the light, the distributions of fortune, what time the milkman gets up, the position of the electron, or the occurrence of one astonishingly frigid winter after another. Even electrons, supposedly the paragons of unpredictability, are tame and obsequious little creatures that rush around at the speed of light, going precisely where they are supposed to go. They make faint whistling sounds that when apprehended in varying combinations are as pleasant as the wind flying through a forest, and they do exactly as they are told. Of this, one can be certain.

And yet there is a wonderful anarchy, in that the milkman chooses when to arise, the rat picks the tunnel into which he will dive when the subway comes rushing down the track from Borough Hall, and the snowflake will fall as it will. How can this be? If nothing is random, and everything is predetermined, how can there be free will? The answer to that is simple. Nothing is predetermined; it is determined, or was determined, or will be determined. No matter, it all happened at once, in less than an instant, and time was invented because we cannot comprehend in one glance the enormous and detailed canvas that we have been given—so we track it, in linear fashion, piece by piece. Time, however, can easily be overcome; not by chasing the light, but by standing back far enough to see it all at once. The universe is still and complete. Everything that ever was, is; everything that ever will be, is—and so on, in all possible combinations. Though in perceiving it we imagine that it is in motion and unfinished, it is quite finished and quite astonishingly beautiful. In the end, or, rather, as things really are, any event, no matter how small, is intimately and sensibly tied to all others. All rivers run full to the sea; those who are apart are brought together; the lost ones are redeemed; the dead come back to life; the perfectly blue days that have begun and ended in golden dimness continue, immobile and accessible; and, when all is perceived in such a way as to obviate time, justice becomes apparent not as something that will be, but as something that is.[2]

[2] Mark Helprin, *Winter's Tale* (New York: Mariner Books; Houghton, Mifflin Harcourt, 2005), 401–2.

Story #8: William James' Dystopian Utopia

James is one of my favorite philosophers, not because he is always right, but because he is always totally honest and totally human, because he thinks with his heart as well as his head. He once gave this piece of advice to a young student of philosophy: "Building up an author's meaning out of separate texts leads nowhere, unless you have first grasped his centre of vision by an act of imagination."[3] What is imagined is always a concrete particular, like a story. Here is one from James' own life. It is from an essay entitled "What Makes a Life Significant?"

> A few summers ago I spent a happy week at the famous Assembly Grounds on the borders of Chautauqua Lake. The moment one treads that sacred enclosure, one feels one's self in an atmosphere of success. Sobriety and industry, intelligence and goodness, orderliness and ideality, prosperity and cheerfulness, pervade the air. It is a serious and studious picnic on a gigantic scale. Here you have a town of many thousands of inhabitants, beautifully laid out in the forest and drained, and equipped with means of satisfying all the necessary lower and most of the superfluous higher wants of man. You have a first-class college in full blast. You have magnificent music—a chorus of seven hundred voices, with possibly the most perfect open-air auditorium in the world. You have every sort of athletic exercise from sailing, rowing, swimming, bicycling, to the ball-field and the more artificial doings which the gymnasium affords. You have kindergartens and model secondary schools. You have general religious services and special club-houses for the several sects. You have perpetually running soda-water

[3] William James, *The Letters of William James*, vol. 2 (CreateSpace, 2015), 355.

fountains, and daily popular lectures by distinguished men. You have the best of company. . . . You have no zymotic diseases, no poverty, no drunkenness, no crime, no police. You have culture, you have kindness, you have cheapness, you have equality, you have the best fruits of what mankind has fought and bled and striven for under the name of civilization for centuries. You have, in short, a foretaste of what human society might be, were it all in the light, with no suffering and no dark corners.

I went in curiosity for a day. I stayed for a week, held spell-bound by the charm and ease of everything, by the middle-class paradise, without a sin, without a victim, without a blot, without a tear.

And yet what was my own astonishment, on emerging into the dark and wicked world again [he lived in New York City and Boston], to catch myself unexpectedly and involuntarily saying: "Ouf! What a relief! Now for something primordial and savage, even though it were as bad as an Armenian massacre, to set the balance straight again. This order is too tame, this culture too second-rate, this goodness too uninspiring. This human drama without a villain or a pang, this community so refined that ice-cream soda-water is the utmost offering it can make to the brute animal in man; this city simmering in the tepid lakeside sun; this atrocious harmlessness of all things,—I cannot abide with them. Let me take my chances again in the big outside worldly wilderness with all its sins and sufferings. There are the heights and depths, the precipices and the steep ideals, the gleams of the awful and the infinite. . . ."

So I meditated. And, first of all, I asked myself what the thing was that was so lacking in this Sabbatical city. . . . (It) is the everlasting battle of the powers of light with those of darkness; with heroism . . . snatching victory from the jaws of death. But in this unspeakable Chautauqua there was no potentiality of death in sight anywhere, and no point of the compass visible from which danger might possibly appear. . . . But what our human emotions seem to require is the sight of the struggle going on.[4]

The modern equivalent of Chautauqua is "The Truman Show". Or *Brave New World*.

What makes the world we live in perfect? Its imperfections. As that great philosopher Yogi Berra said, "If this world was perfect, it wouldn't be."

If the world is really a paradise, as Dostoyevsky will claim in our next story, it is a "paradise" that is full of sin and suffering. Sin constricts souls. But suffering stretches souls. We need to be stretched.

Story #9: The "Ridiculous" Point of The Brothers Karamazov

Dostoyevsky's novel *The Brothers Karamazov* is almost one thousand pages long and probably the greatest novel ever written. Its central philosophical idea is summarized in a few pages, in the teachings of Father Zossima as collected by his disciple, the Karamazov brother Dostoyevsky calls his "hero", Alyosha. Father Zossima, in turn, learned it from his dying seventeen-year-old brother, Markel. This chain of witnesses is put in to suggest that the idea is not original; it is not Dostoyevsky's invention; it is a common point in Christian mysticism, especially Orthodox mysticism. The Russian word for it, *sobornost*, cannot be perfectly translated

---

[4] William James, *On Some of Life's Ideals; On a Certain Blindness in Human Beings; What Makes a Life Significant* (Eastford, Conn.: Martino Fine Books, 2016), 53–58.

into English. It combines many meanings into one. Some of those meanings, and translations, are: "friendship", "relationship", "oneness", "universality", "wholeness", "community", "family", "togetherness", "withness", and "city" (in Augustine's sense of *civitas*: an invisible society of persons unified by a common end, a common love).

Dostoyevsky's vision of *sobornost* can be summarized in four apparently ridiculous teachings, which constitute a metaphysics, an epistemology, a cosmology, and an ethics. The four parts are four dimensions of a single vision. The epistemology is a consequence of the metaphysics, and the ethics is a consequence of the cosmology.

1. Metaphysics: *"We are all in paradise, but we don't see it."*

2. Epistemology: *"If you love everything, you will perceive the divine mystery."*

3. Cosmology: *"A touch in one place sets up movement at the other end of the earth."*

4. Ethics: *"We are all responsible to all and for all."*

The metaphysical point is so startling that it seems at first psychologically insane and religiously heretical. How can earth be (literally) Heaven, especially to a young boy who is dying in great pain?

> Mother would go to her room and weep, but when she went in to him she wiped her eyes and looked cheerful. "Mother, don't weep, darling," he would say, "I've long to live yet, long to rejoice with you, and life is glad and joyful."
>
> "Ah, dear boy, how can you talk of joy when you lie feverish at night, coughing as though you would tear yourself to pieces."

"Don't cry, mother," he would answer, "life is paradise, and we are all in paradise, but we won't see it; if we would, we should have heaven on earth the next day."

Everyone wondered at his words, he spoke so strangely and positively; we were all touched and wept. . . .

"And another thing, mother, every one of us has sinned against all men, and I more than any."

Mother positively smiled at that, smiled through her tears. "Why, how could you have sinned against all men, more than all? Robbers and murderers have done that, but what sin have you committed yet, that you hold yourself more guilty than all?"

"Mother, little heart of mine," he said (he had begun using such strange caressing words at that time), "little heart of mine, my joy, believe me, everyone is really responsible to all men for all men and for everything. . . ."

"Your son cannot last long," the doctor told my mother, as she accompanied him to the door. "The disease is affecting his brain."

The windows of his room looked out into the garden, and our garden was a shady one, with old trees in it which were coming into bud. The first birds of spring were flitting in the branches, chirruping and singing at the windows. And looking at them and admiring them, he began suddenly begging their forgiveness too: "Birds of heaven, happy birds, forgive me, for I have sinned against you too." None of us could understand that at the time, but he shed tears of joy. "Yes," he said, "there was such a glory of God all about me: birds, trees, meadows, sky; only I lived in shame and dishonoured it all and did not notice the beauty and glory."

"You take too many sins on yourself," mother used to say, weeping.

"Mother, darling, it's for joy, not for grief I am crying. Though I can't explain it to you. I like to humble myself before them, for I don't know how to love them enough. If I have sinned against everyone, yet all forgive me, too, and that's heaven. Am I not in heaven now?"[5]

Years later, Father Zossima taught this philosophy to a "mysterious visitor", who believed it even more readily than Father Zossima did:

"That life is heaven," he said to me suddenly, "that I have long been thinking about"; and all at once he added, "I think of nothing else indeed." He looked at me and smiled. "I am more convinced of it than you are. . . . Heaven . . . lies hidden within all of us—here it lies hidden in me now, and if I will it, it will be revealed to me tomorrow and for all time."

I looked at him; he was speaking with great emotion and gazing mysteriously at me, as if he were questioning me.

"And that we are all responsible to all for all, apart from our own sins, you were quite right in thinking that, and it is wonderful how you could comprehend it in all its significance at once. And in very truth, so soon as men understand that, the Kingdom of Heaven will be for them not a dream, but a living reality."[6]

Father Zossima's later teaching confirmed this Heavenly vision of a universal, cosmic spiritual gravity. If gravity is "the love that moves the sun and the other stars", if all matter is in love with all matter, why is not all spirit in love with all spirit? We live in a universe, not a pluriverse; why should this not be as true of spirit as of matter?

Every hour and every moment thousands of men leave life on this earth, and their souls appear before God. And how many of them depart in solitude, unknown, sad, dejected

[5] Fyodor Dostoyevsky, *The Karamazov Brothers*, trans. Constance Garnett (London: Wordsworth Editions, 2007), 316–17.
[6] Ibid., 333–35.

that no one mourns for them or even knows whether they have lived or not. And behold, from the other end of the earth perhaps, your prayer for their rest will rise up to God though you knew them not nor they you. . . .

Love a man even in his sin, for that is the semblance of Divine Love and is the highest love on earth. Love all God's creation, the whole and every grain of sand in it. Love every leaf, every ray of God's light. Love the animals, love the plants, love everything. If you love everything, you will perceive the divine mystery in things. . . . Love is a teacher; but one must know how to acquire it, for it is hard to acquire, it is dearly bought, it is won slowly by long labour. For we must love not only occasionally, for a moment, but for ever. Everyone can love occasionally, even the wicked can.

My brother asked the birds to forgive him; that sounds senseless, but it is right; for all is like an ocean, all is flowing and blending; a touch in one place sets up movement at the other end of the earth. It may be senseless to beg forgiveness of the birds, but birds would be happier at your side —a little happier, anyway—and children and all animals, if you yourself were nobler than you are now. It's all like an ocean, I tell you. . . .

Take yourself and make yourself responsible for all men's sins, that is the truth, you know, friends, for as soon as you sincerely make yourself responsible for everything and for all men, you will see at once that it is really so, and that you are to blame for everyone and for all things. . . .

Remember particularly that you cannot be a judge of anyone. For no one can judge a criminal until he recognises that he is just such a criminal as the man standing before him, and that he perhaps is more than all men to blame for that crime. When he understands that, he will be able to be a judge. Though that sounds absurd, it is true. If I had been righteous myself, perhaps there would have been no criminal standing before me.[7]

There are four claims in this vision. The first (the metaphysical claim that we are all in paradise now, we just don't see it) and the last (the ethical claim that we are each responsible for all, for all sins) are the most startling. The third (the cosmological claim of *sobornost*, the spiritual gravity or, to use Dostoyevsky's image, the spiritual "ocean") is the basis for both of these truths. That's what makes earth Heaven and what makes every spiritual atom in it a partial causal influence on, and therefore partly responsible for, every other spiritual atom. (The Greek word for "cause", *aition*, means "responsibility", as in a court trial.) And the second point —the epistemological claim that we do not see this *because we do not love*; that love in the heart opens this vision in the mind—this is the way to test and prove the whole vision, the whole four claims, to yourself. Try it; you'll like it!

Story #10: H.G. Wells' "The Door in the Wall"

All these stories reveal what I have called "doors" in the "walls" of the world, so it is fitting that we end with a story about those two very symbols. Ironically, it is written by a man who did not believe in transcendence or the supernatural. Wells was an atheist (or, perhaps at a deeper level, an agnostic), a scientific materialist, and a secular left-wing Utopian Socialist whose *Outline of History* blamed the Church for most of the evils in the world. Yet there was a soft, childlike side to him, too, which was evident in the

[7] Ibid., 352–55.

Christlike symbolism in "The Selfish Giant" and in a surprisingly open-to-religion short story called "The Door in the Wall".

The two symbols are obvious: the wall is the visible world of matter, and the door through it leads to another world, a Heaven, a Paradise. Thus the Door is the most important thing in the world, the ultimate end and meaning of life. The wall is white (the color of ghosts, of Great White sharks, and of Moby Dick), and the door is green (the color of life and hope). The story is narrated by a skeptic and agnostic, which was Wells' public face, but the story within the story is told by a man named Wallace, who is the other half of Wells, a man who discovered that there was indeed a door in the wall. As a five-year-old, he found it, on a familiar West Kensington road, dared to open it and go through, and found a Paradise. Inside, a wise old woman showed him his life in a picture book whose pages she turned. As soon as they came to the present, he found himself on the street outside the door, which he could not find again. When he told his story to his family and friends, they reviled him and punished him. He knew it was not a dream, but no one else knew that, including the narrator (Wells), who began and ended with doubts.

Wallace found the door again only three times later in his adult life, but each appearance came at a crucial time when he had to choose between worldly ambitions and a return to Paradise. All three times, he passed the door by and bitterly regretted it later. At the end, he died by falling into an excavation that he reached through a door in the wall that protected it. The author, however, is not quite convinced that the Door was only an illusion after all. And neither, apparently, was Wells.

And neither can anyone else be. How can the fetus know there is no world outside the womb? How can the bottom-dwelling fish know there is no sky? How can the prisoners know there is no escape from the cave?

II

The Setting:
The Fragility of Time

This chapter will be short because the setting is the least important of the five dimensions of a story. Yet it makes a difference to the whole, in fact, a difference that is essential. Shakespeare's *Romeo and Juliet* becomes a different story when *West Side Story* changes the setting to twentieth-century New York City, even though the plots and themes are the same.

In the last three books of his *Confessions*, Augustine steps back from the story of his life that he has just told and thinks hard about time, our memory that transcends present time, and God's creation of time. For *time is the setting* of that story and of all stories.

He begins with the necessary beginning, Socratic humility and ignorance, and famously says that if no one asks us what time is, we all know what it is, but when anyone asks us, we discover that we don't really know what it is. And neither does anyone else.

This is Socratic, for only by critiquing our former opinions can we hope to move forward to a truer view. So what are our usual false opinions about time?

We usually think of it under two assumptions. First of

all, we divide it into past, present, and future, and we think of the present as the moment that divides time in two by distinguishing past from future, like a point on a line dividing the line into two parts.

Second, time seems to be a purely material thing that our mind discovers rather than creates: it seems to be the mere movement of matter through space.

But these two assumptions break down when we think about them. (Saint Augustine first discovered this.) First of all, if we think of time as a kind of line, with the present being merely the dividing point between past and future, then only past and future remain as parts of that line, and the present disappears, because a point has no width at all. And that is not all: what is left, the past and future, also disappears, because the past is already dead and the future is not yet born. What has happened in this false analysis is that the unreal past and future have mastered and devoured the real present. We must reverse this, so that the real present masters and devours, or rather creates, the past and the future: the past by memory and the future by anticipation or desire. Of course our mind does not create the events of the past or the future, but it does create the pastness of the past and the futureness of the future. For the past is what is looked back on by a present consciousness and the future is what is looked forward to by a present consciousness.

Second, time involves not only material events but also a mind measuring these events as past and future through the present acts of remembering and anticipating.

So everything real is present, for even pastness and futureness are constituted, or made, by the present, *and by our consciousness.*

What does this have to do with the doors in the wall of Plato's Cave?

As we saw in our Introduction, human consciousness is supernatural in relation to matter. The knowledge of matter is not a part of matter, not a material particle. Thus time, the dimension of the universe that is the most ubiquitously imminent to both matter and mind is also the most ubiquitously transcendent. At every moment, it is a door out of the universe of matter and into another universe, the universe of mind, consciousness, human reason, or thinking, that is supernatural in relation to matter.

However, human thinking is time-bound, since it is the moving present, not God's unchanging present, and therefore although it is supernatural in relation to matter, it is also natural in relation to God, who is timeless. Human thinking, unlike divine thinking, is in time. But it is not merely in material time (*kronos*), the time that is measured by the movement of matter through space, but it is in spiritual time (*kairos*), which is measured by memory and by purpose and hope and desire and intention and plan, that is, by mind and meaning.

Those are just some definitions and therefore dull; but here comes the consequence, which is startling. Since human thinking is in time and divine thinking is not; and since it is human thinking that creates the pastness of the past and the futureness of the future; and since it is divine thinking rather than human thinking that is the standard for what is real; what follows is the startling conclusion that this pastness and futureness, this *kairos-time* that measures the movements of the human spirit in its values and purposes, like the *kronos-time* that measures the movements of matter through space, is not independently real, not *ultimately* real—that is, not real from God's point of view, only from ours. As Mark Helprin said, we invented time because we could not take in the whole painting of all the events in history at once from a viewpoint outside of it, as the spectator of a painting does when he looks at the painting as a whole on the wall, because we are not spectators of this painting that is history, we are parts of it; we are in process of making it. But God sees it all at once, and what God sees is real; therefore, its all-at-once-ness is real. More real than time.

And therefore time can be overcome—not destroyed, but overcome. Time's negativities, time's separations, time's train whistles in the night that always mean that somebody is saying goodbye—that is overcome. As Tom Howard writes,

> Behold I make all things new. Behold I do what cannot be done. I restore the years that the locusts and worms have eaten. I restore the years which you have drooped away upon your crutches and in your wheelchair. I restore the symphonies and operas which your deaf ears have never heard and the snowy massif your blind eyes have never seen, and the freedom lost to you through plunder, and the identity lost to you because of calumny and the failure of justice; and I restore the good which your own foolish mistakes have cheated you of. And I bring you to the Love of which all other loves speak, the Love which is joy and beauty, and which you have sought in a thousand streets and for which you have wept and clawed your pillow.[1]

God said this to us in the last chapter of the last book of the Bible and the last chapter of human history; and in *The Passion of Christ*, Christ said it to his mother on the Via Dolorosa, in the greatest line in the history of cinema: "See, Mother, I make all things new."

The Cave is not abolished as an illusion, a *maya*, as in some forms of ancient Eastern mysticism. Nor is it absolutized, as in modern Western materialism. It is renovated. It

---

[1] Thomas Howard, *Christ the Tiger* (Eugene, Ore.: Wipf & Stock, 2004), 133.

is made into a king's palace. The very wounds of Christ are transformed into badges of glory in His resurrected body. The very darkest tragedies of time are seen as brilliancies in the light of eternity. For the darkest deed of all, the deliberate murder of Almighty God, has become something Christians celebrate as "*Good* Friday". Moral evil has not become moral good, but all other kinds of evil have become goods, or shown themselves to have been goods all along, or to have worked together for good (Rom 8:28). The worst thing has become the best thing. Death has become our door to Life. Down has become an Up. Suffering has become joy. Time is so fragile and defenseless that "Death itself would start working backward."[2]

In George MacDonald's classic fairy tale "The Golden Key", the Old Man of the Sea asks Mossy, who has died and returned to life, whether death is good; and Mossy answers, "It is better than life", to which the Old Man then responds, "No. It is only more life."[3] When Saint Paul asked a similar question, he gave a similar answer: "For to me to live is Christ, and [therefore] to die is gain"—because it is only more Christ.

Not only is time not part of the wall but it is itself a door in the wall. Time transcends itself.

So in the setting as well as in the plot (and, as we shall see, in the characters, the theme, and the style, too), this is truly "the greatest story ever told". This is part of Gospel, of "good news". Truly, "there is no tale ever told that men would rather find was true."[4]

[2] C. S. Lewis, *The Last Battle* (New York: HarperCollins, 2001), 185.

[3] George MacDonald, *The Golden Key* (Grand Rapids, Mich.: Eerdmans, 2016), 112.

[4] J. R. R. Tolkien, *Tolkien on Fairy-Stories*, ed. Verlyn Flieger and Douglas A. Anderson (London: HarperCollins, 2008), 78.

III

The Characters: The Real
Presence of Invisible Friends

We find life's meaning, as we find our own identities, only in the presence of other persons, that is, in relationships. Buber wrote in *I and Thou*: "All real living is meeting." Marcel wrote in "On the Ontological Mystery": "For man, to be is to be in relation; *esse est co-esse* (to be is to be-with)." This principle goes "all the way up" into the Trinity.

Who are these others, these friends and neighbors of ours? We have not only visible friends (each other) but also invisible friends in four possible categories. The first, of course, is God, Who is our Very Best Friend. Why in the world God, the perfect Being who has no needs whatever, wants to be not only in relationship with but friends with the likes of us stupid, silly, shallow, sinful creatures surpasses all human knowing; but that is the Good News of the world's most popular and beloved Book.

Of all the characters in the story, He is the most interesting. (After all, how could any or all of the characters be more interesting than their Author? The effect cannot exceed the cause.) When He became incarnate and entered into His own story as its main character (after all, a human author can do that; why can't a divine Author?), He did a number of things no other man ever did, such as (1) fulfilling hundreds of prophecies about Him; (2) claiming to be God and yet not being either a liar or a lunatic; (3) performing far more miracles than any other human being ever did; and (4) rising from the dead. Another one of those unique things, seldom noticed, is this: Jesus was the only person who ever lived who never bored anybody. If he were an invented fictional character, he was by far the most interesting character in the history of fiction. And what human author invented this unparalleled fiction? A confused gaggle of Galilean fishermen? Or, much later, a committee of crafty theologians? If you can believe that, you have far more faith than I have.

A second category of invisible friends is the angels, who surround us, vastly outnumber us, and greatly (but not infinitely) surpass us in intelligence, goodwill, and power. (God infinitely surpasses both us and them in all three of those divine attributes.) At every important turn of events in the Bible, they are there.

There are also evil angels, fallen angels, demons, devils, or evil spirits. They are mere superstitions if and only if all the religions, saints, sages, and scriptures of every culture and every religion in the entire history of the world are silly, stupid, and deluded, and we alone, we modern, uprooted snobs, are wise. They do not show up in test tubes—but neither does God.

A third category of friends is comprised of the saints in Heaven. They are still human, but they are so *perfectly* human now that if we saw them without the veils between us that divine mercy provides to our blessed ignorance, we would be so dazzled that we would be tempted to fall down and worship them, or at least be so confused that we would babble nonsense, as Saint Peter did on the Mount of Transfiguration.

A fourth category of invisible friends is only a possibility, but it is worth imagining: other intelligent species of creatures, on other planets in our universe. They are part of the universe, thus not really supernatural, but they are super-terrestrial, extraterrestrial. They do not interact with us in our story, or at least have not yet done so, as far as we know. (Or *do* we know? What about Bill "Spaceman" Lee and Dennis Rodman?)

A few words about each of these categories of characters.

1. God

If God does not exist, then life is "full of sound and fury, signifying nothing". For if life is a story, there must be a Storyteller. Is that us? Can the characters be the Author?

The reasonableness of the No answer to that question is the fundamental reason why the Bible is the most popular book in the world.

Let's be totally candid: Isn't it ridiculous that the Bible is the most popular book in the world? It is messy (like life). It is not neat, clear, nicely ordered, or even, apparently, very reasonable. The primitive parts of it are (surprise, surprise) very primitive. On a human level, that is, in the minds of all its human authors and readers as distinct from the Mind of God, it is a hodgepodge of wildly different books, styles, genres, personalities, assumptions, points, and purposes. Its unity is not apparent. Insofar as it does have a unity (we might call this unity "Stories about God"), its unifying point sounds utterly crazy: that there is an absolutely perfect Being who needs nothing but who nevertheless bothers enormously about us radically imperfect beings, and unpredictably interferes with our lives because for some utterly unintelligible reason He loves us—even though the data of our lives strongly seem to refute this hypothesis ("the problem of evil"). The reason this book is the most popular book in the world cannot possibly be its artistic unity and coherence, its apparent rationality, or its fitting in with our expectations. It is not our own wishful thinking because if we invented a religion, we certainly would not invent one that included Hell. It is not our own pessimistic or cynical thinking because if we invented a cynical religion, we certainly would not invent such a good God or such a happy Heaven. Pessimists might invent a pessimistic religion, optimists an optimistic religion, and meliorists a boring, middle-of-the-road, commonsense religion, but who would ever invent a religion that included both Hell and Heaven, both sin and salvation, both justice and mercy?

The reason for its popularity is the same as the reason for the popularity of any great novel: its protagonist, its central character, is a real *character.*

But this book claims to be fact, not fiction. This book announces that the most important Fact is an invisible, eternal, all-powerful, all-wise, and all-good God who is The Main Thing on the other side of all the doors in the walls of the world. He is not just more, but infinitely more, than the sum total of all other things in existence. We cannot know what He is, only what He is not. His essence is unknowable, and He "dwells in inaccessible light". And this God is our Friend and Lover(!?).

"Too good to be true?" That is certainly what it looks like when we first compare the hypothesis with the data, when we compare the basic claim of this most famous book with what appears in our daily experience. If there is a God who is all-good, then He must will only what is good for all His creatures, especially us. And if He is all-wise, He must know exactly and infallibly what is for our best good. And if He is the all-powerful Creator of the entire universe, then He must have the power to make all things work together for our best good if we only freely choose to let Him. (Therefore only the double presupposition of our free will and our ignorance could explain the existence of all the evil in the world.) But that conclusion, that "all things work together for good to them that love God" (Rom 8:28 KJV), that conclusion that is the logically necessary result of the three non-negotiable theistic premises of God's unlimited goodness, wisdom, and power, certainly does not look like a fact. It looks far, far "too good to be true". So why is this book so popular?

Because the only logically possible alternative to this crazy world view, this package deal, is that it is indeed too good to be true; that it is our supreme wish-fulfillment fantasy. But in that case, if it is really "too good to be true", then our two deepest needs and desires, Goodness and Truth, contradict each other. In that case, at the deep center of every human heart, there is a self-contradiction.

You can believe that if you want to, and you can also believe the opposite if you want to. Each is logically possible. You pay your money, and you take your choice.

It is not evident, not obvious, which of these two philosophies of life is true. We do not have the "over the top" perspective of the eagle or the angel. We do not look down on life from above.

But we do have the perspective of the characters in the story. We do not know God's mind, but we do know our own lives. And if we compare the *results* in our own lives of believing each of these two world views, that difference is evident, is obvious; and that difference is evidence, is *data*. We do not have divine data, but we have human data. And that data, I think, is the main reason why this strange Book is the most popular book in the world. The data I'm talking about are saints. Saints are the most interesting people, the most creative people, the most trustable people, the most happy people in the world. Mother Teresa was radiantly happy, even though she lived in an almost lifelong "dark night of the soul". Simone de Beauvoir was not. The Madonna is happy. Madonna is not. The martyrs were happy. Nero was not. Those are data. Those are the loose threads on our backside of the tapestry. Millions of threads.

Millions of threads can make up a rope. A rope strong enough to pull a ship through a storm, if you let it, if you trust it, if you use it.

2. Angels

The same book also announces that there are innumerable angels, invisible and immaterial persons (i.e., beings with intellects and wills) surrounding us and inspiring us and guiding us and guarding us, fighting for us—invisible warriors. They are always there, but God rarely lifts the curtain that blinds our eyes to them, as he did to Elisha's servant, in a passage that gives me chills every time I read it. The King of Syria sends his army to kill the prophet Elisha, and

> It was told him, "Behold, he is in Dothan." So he sent there horses and chariots and a great army; and they came by night, and surrounded the city. When the servant of the man of God rose early in the morning and went out, behold, an army with horses and chariots was round about the city. And the servant said, "Alas, my master! What shall we do?" He [Elisha] said, "Fear not, for those who are with us are more than those who are with them." Then Elisha

prayed, and said, "O LORD, I beg you, open his eyes that he may see." So the LORD opened the eyes of the young man, and he saw; and behold, the mountain was full of horses and chariots of fire round about Elisha. (1 Kings 6:13–17)

God did not put this vision into Elisha's servant's eyes or mind; he merely removed the blinders from his eyes so that he could see what was just as truly and factually *there* as the nose on his face. And this story is not the exception but the rule. The angels do not sleep. They are always there.

If we look at the story not just from the viewpoint of the "good guys" (Elisha and his servant) but from the viewpoint of the "bad guys" (the king and his soldiers), we will feel the deeper *frisson:* even when we surround, we are surrounded. Even when we watch, we are being watched. There are Eyes outside our windows. We are running a race, and the runners are outnumbered by the spectators in the stands. These spectators are both angels and saints.

3. Saints

Though only suggested in the Old Testament, it is made clear in the New Testament that saints and martyrs are added to the divine and angelic witnesses. They are sitting still in eternity watching us run our race in the stadium of Time: "Therefore, since we are surrounded by so great a cloud of witnesses . . . let us run with endurance the race that is set before us" (Heb 12:1).

The wonder at recognizing this company of witnesses and the awe it evokes surpass even that in the Old Testament:

> For you have not come to what may be touched, a blazing fire, and darkness, and gloom, and a tempest, and the sound

of a trumpet, and a voice whose words made the hearers entreat that no further messages be spoken to them. For they could not endure the order that was given, "If even a beast touches the mountain, it shall be stoned." Indeed, so terrifying was the sight that Moses said, "I tremble with fear." But you have come to Mount Zion and to the city of the living God, the heavenly Jerusalem, and to innumerable angels in festal gathering, and to the assembly of the first-born who are enrolled in heaven, and to a judge who is God of all, and to the spirits of just men made perfect, and to Jesus, the mediator of a new covenant, and to the sprinkled blood that speaks more graciously than the blood of Abel. See that you do not refuse him who is speaking. For if they did not escape when they refused him who warned them on earth, much less shall we escape if we reject him who warns us from heaven. His voice then shook the earth; but now he has promised, "Yet once more I will shake not only the earth but also the heaven." This phrase, "Yet once more," indicates the removal of what is shaken, as of what has been made, in order that what cannot be shaken may remain. Therefore let us be grateful for receiving a kingdom that cannot be shaken, and thus let us offer to God acceptable worship, with reverence and awe; for our God is a consuming fire. (Heb 12:18–29)

The disciples saw this heavenly glory when they saw the divinity of Christ coming out of hiding behind His human nature at the Transfiguration. His face did not reflect light; it generated it. They saw the Source of all the light in the world; they saw with their eyes the One who was the constant in Einstein's great equation.

Catholics see the same thing, though only by the "eyes" of faith, under the humblest of appearances (bread and wine) in the Eucharist.

4. Extraterrestrials?

So we are in the presence of (1) God, (2) His angels, and (3) the saints, and (4) maybe even extraterrestrials, if there are any. Of course this last group is highly speculative. But just to expand our minds and open our imaginations, let's tell a story. It is fiction, of course, but if it were even remotely possible, it would put another crack in the walls of our little cave.

PILGRIMAGE

You will not believe my story. As I grope for words, I am painfully aware that none will suffice. The experience was so unfamiliar that I despair of communicating it in familiar English words as I put them on familiar white paper.

I know it happened, but I do not know how it happened, whether by a power divine, angelic, demonic, merely human, or something else. Nor do I know why it happened to me.

I was in Jerusalem, on pilgrimage to the usual Christian shrines. I was alone, not in a group. I was fulfilling my life-long dream to "walk today where Jesus walked".

It was Christmas Day, and of course I wanted to be in Bethlehem. I had decided to walk from my hotel in Jerusalem down the few miles of well-traveled road to Bethlehem. Somehow a bus seemed the wrong vehicle for a pilgrimage. But I was about to meet some pilgrims who had used a far stranger vehicle than a bus.

I had been disappointed by many of the shrines I had visited—or perhaps I was only disappointed with my own disappointment, my own curmudgeon-like reaction to their commercialization. I had felt nothing mystical or profound or even very spiritual the last few days and was not feeling any of those things that day. At the end of the long walk, I felt only tired, nothing more. Nothing prepared me for what came next.

What happened was not that something new was added to the world but that something old was subtracted. I felt as if blinders had been taken off my eyes, like Elisha's servant (in the previous story). I saw—but how can I possibly tell you what I saw? It was not a vision. It was a Thing. We do not see a vision; a vision is the act of seeing something. My means of seeing were not changed. They were my eyes, my same old eyes. It was *what* I saw that was different. Utterly different.

What I saw was not God, not angels, and not saints. It was creatures. Rational creatures, rational animals, like us, but utterly unlike us. They were other species. *Many* other species. I will not try to describe them in detail, because if I did, you would focus on the strangeness of the details and you would lose the strangeness of the whole thing. It would be like watching the cantina scene from the movie *Star Wars*. But it was not like that. I cannot tell you what it was like. But it was not like that. It was not like a movie, a daydream, a dream, a nightmare, or an act of imagination.

As I approached the shrine that commemorates the place where Jesus is supposed to have been born, I saw thousands of creatures hovering around it. I call them "creatures", but they were not animals, humans, saints, or angels. They were utterly alien entities. I knew that they were intensely *aware*. I do not know *how* I knew that. They did not see me—or if they did, they paid no attention to me. They were focused on the same spot on which I was focused, the spot where Jesus was born.

They were like me in only one way: they, too, were on pilgrimage.

Each was performing some action. Some of these actions were visible: twirling, sending out pulsations of light, moving parts of their bodies. Some of them were still with a stillness that was more alive than any motion.

There were hundreds of other human pilgrims surrounding the site, but no one else seemed aware of the aliens except me. I have no idea why I was selected to see what no one else in the history of the world ever saw, since there is absolutely nothing remarkable about me in any way. (Perhaps that is the reason?) After I came home, I spent hundreds of hours searching and researching every arcane source I could find for any hint of an experience similar to mine, but I found nothing.

Upon reflection, one thing that strikes me as strange now (though not at the time) was that the bodies of these aliens *overlapped*. There were many thousands of them there, and our physical laws say that two bodies cannot occupy the same space at the same time. But other laws than those of physics must have governed whatever was happening there and then. These were real bodies, not holograms or visions —I am sure of that, though I do not know how to prove it to you—yet they were overlapping in space. I saw each "layer" of bodies with equal clarity, the ones "overlapped" as well as the ones "overlapping", and the ones behind as clearly as the ones in front. None were ghostlike; all were solid.

After a time whose length I have totally forgotten, something else happened. I felt another mind touching mine. It said nothing. It was not "mental telepathy" in the sense of a communication of information, but a Seeing that touched my seeing so that I could "see" what it saw or know what it knew. It was a kind of timeless transfer without words, but in order to tell it, I must put it into time and into words.

My first question was: "Are they really there?" And the answer came instantly and indubitably. It was: "They are there just as truly as you are there." But what I here call the "answer" did not come after the question, even though it was a set of words, one *after* the other. (I don't understand how that can be, but that's how it appeared to me.)

I next wondered why their bodies cast no shadows and disturbed no dust, and the instant answer was silence. The question sailed nowhere; it sank as soon as it was launched from my dock.

I then "asked" where they had come from, and the answer was simply: "From their homes." I interpreted this to mean they were from other planets, although this was not part of the answer but only my interpretation.

Then I was made to understand, without asking, that all these creatures had *died*. That was almost as surprising as their appearance, for the distance between life and death is greater than the distance from one galaxy to another.

My next question concerned the nature of their post-mortem bodies, and this question also sank instantly into the great silence. I was digressing. I was made to feel I had to learn something else. I had to focus.

I then asked a "stupid" question that proved to be the right one: What were they all doing here? And the answer came very loud and clear: they were *worshipping*. As I was. Worshipping the same God. They, too, were on pilgrimage.

Without asking the question, I knew that they had not come by spaceship. The dead do not need our transportation systems.

I then asked a theological question: Were these races fallen like ours or unfallen? And the answer that I heard, or saw, was that they all were as innocent as unfallen Eve. None had come to this place by my road, the long, hard, painful road of rebellion and repentance.

Then I asked whether the Son of God had come to their planets as He had come to ours. This was a question somewhat like the one that had divided the theologians in the Middle Ages: If Man had not fallen, would God have become incarnate? And the answer was both a yes and a no: he had come to these other planets, but not to die. It was not clear to me whether He had incarnated himself in alien bodies or not, but when I think and compare the "yes" and the "no" answers to that question, the "no" has a strong sense of seeming, or *smelling,* right. But I may well be wrong about that. But if I am right, then the old pre-Copernican geocentrism was right in a spiritual sense. We earthlings were indeed at the center of the universe because the Son of God had been born to die here and here alone. That was why all other races came on pilgrimage here.

I finally asked the question I was supposed to ask: What am I supposed to learn from this? And the "answer" was that I was supposed to learn *where I am.* I was in Bethlehem, of course. But where was Bethlehem? Physically, it was in Israel, a little west of Jerusalem. Spiritually, it was at the center of the universe. For "Bethlehem" means "House of Bread". Bethlehem is the spiritual kitchen for the world, where the bread of the world was baked, where the Body that was to be given up in death for our salvation was born. No other world needed such a bread because no other world had eaten the forbidden bread, the forbidden fruit. We were the object of attention and pilgrimage for the entire universe. We were both the pity and the envy of the universe because of our unique sin and God's unique response. O felix culpa!

When I expressed my surprise (wordlessly) at this paradox, I was reminded of the parable of the lost sheep. The Good Shepherd left the ninety-nine obedient sheep at home to seek and find the one who was lost. Now I realized who these ninety-nine were. I was seeing them.

I also saw the greater meaning of the prophecy of the Gentiles making pilgrimages to Jerusalem. I had always interpreted "Gentiles" as earth's non-Jewish Christians, but these aliens were the cosmic Gentiles.

Then, as suddenly as the vision had appeared, it disappeared. All was as it had been. Or rather, nothing was as it had been. My cave had been opened.

I returned to my familiar little world and have lived normally ever since. But I can never forget for a single second two things about the world I live in: how tiny it is compared with the myriads of other worlds and races, and how precious it is because it alone contains the holiest place in the universe, the womb that contained the Creator.

Upon reflection, this is not so surprising because the divine style and strategy are always to go, like water, to the lowest place, the driest and neediest place. The Creator became, not one of *them*, but one of us; and among us He chose, not Rome or Athens or even Jerusalem, but Bethlehem and, then, Nazareth. The first terrestrial pilgrims, the shepherds, followed Him there: "Let us go now down to Bethlehem." Not up, but down. God came down, so how could we do less? The extraterrestrial pilgrims did the same.

And so must we go down to Bethlehem, to Calcutta, to Iowa, and even down to the expensive high-rise skyscrapers that are some of the lowest places on earth, the spiritual Dead Sea. For He is there, too, as our bread. All places are Bethlehems. The vision was given to teach me, not about aliens, but about ourselves.

IV

The Theme: Joy

What is the theme of our story? What is its "moral"? What is "the meaning of life"? There are many ways of answering that question: being a good person, leading a good life, treating others with justice, kindness, and respect—and although these are not necessarily religious answers, they are not wrong answers. Faith, hope, and charity (*agapē* love), the three "theological virtues" that glue us to our final end, are the religious answers, and they do not exclude but include the other ones. In a way, they are not "other" but dimensions of one and the same answer: that the meaning of our life is to become Godlike, and that is not just one option among many because God is not one god among many.

But what do we get, what do we find, what do we become, what happens to us when we find those answers, that answer, or that Answer?

Philosophers and psychologists from Aristotle to Freud have replied: *Happiness.*

Everyone wants happiness and fears unhappiness or misery. Aristotle, the philosopher of common sense, knew that. In fact, everyone knows that, even Freud, even though Freud, like Epicurus and John Stuart Mill and all other materialists, identified happiness with pleasure.

Whether happiness is merely pleasure, as Freud says, or something much more, as Aristotle says; and whether that requires material goods or not; and whether it is objective goodness as well as subjective satisfaction; everyone seeks happiness for its own sake, not as a means to any other end; and everyone seeks everything else as a means to happiness or as an ingredient in happiness.

But what is happiness?

The question is not what things make us happy but what is the psychological state that we seek as our final, deepest end.

The typically modern answer is that happiness is simply contentment, the satisfaction of all our desires. But that is not the deepest thing we seek, for that proves boring. (Remember William James' Chautauqua!) We seek more than contentment; we seek joy.

Joy is supernatural. Joy is a door in the wall. Pleasure and happiness are not necessarily doors to the supernatural, but joy is.

But what is joy?

1. What Is Joy?

We share pleasure with animals. Happiness raises us above the animals and above pleasure. But joy raises us above ourselves.

We can understand the difference between joy and happiness best if we first understand the difference between happiness and pleasure.

Everyone wants pleasure and hates pain. And everyone knows that, even Freud, who reduced everything else to it ("the pleasure principle").

There are at least four differences between happiness and

pleasure. (1) Happiness is more interior than pleasure. (2) It is more invisible and mysterious than pleasure. (3) It is less controllable than pleasure. (4) And it is more lasting than pleasure.

Joy is to happiness what happiness is to pleasure. (1) It is more interior than happiness; it is a matter of the deep secret at the heart of the heart. (2) It is more invisible and mysterious than happiness. (3) It is even less controllable than happiness. In fact, happiness *is* controllable in its most important part (the soul); that is one of life's great lessons: that you are responsible for your own happiness; that it is the practice of the virtues that makes you happy. (4) Joy is not, however, more lasting in this life than happiness. It comes suddenly and leaves almost as suddenly, like an alien in a flying saucer. It is a brief appetizer, not a lasting meal.

Pleasure is sunny-yellow; happiness is sky-blue, joy is flaming red.

Or pleasure is green, like grass; happiness is brown, like the fur of a dog; joy is purple, like a wizard's robe.

Or pleasure is white; happiness is silver; joy is gold.

Pleasure is to the heart what sense experience is to the head. Happiness is to the heart what knowledge is to the head. Joy is to the heart what wisdom and understanding are to the head. It is at the bottom.

The heart is a grand canyon. The north rim (the mind) and the south rim (the heart) meet at the bottom, where the River flows. At the surface, the two rims are far apart: sensory data and pleasure. Halfway down, the sides are closer together: knowledge and happiness. At the bottom, the two become almost one: wisdom and joy. Wisdom and joy are the two banks of the River. The River has no name, because it is "mystical". It comes from outside the canyon. It is the living water of God's own life. It wears down the rocks of the soul, the hard human heart and head, to make it into an open canyon. Even in the world of matter, rock has no defense against water.

We all want joy, just as we all want pleasure and happiness; but not everyone knows that, because not everyone knows what joy is. For everyone has experienced pleasure and happiness, but not everyone has experienced joy.

Happiness can get boring, because it is the satisfaction of our desires, and we know what we desire. (Can you desire what you do not know?) Joy never gets boring because it transcends our desires and surprises them with gifts. The Giver of these gifts is invisible, indefinable, and usually unknown. Thus we sometimes speak of "joy without a cause". Nothing in time is without any cause at all, but some things are without a detectable cause.

Happiness is partly controllable, as pleasure is; joy is always a surprise, a gift.

Happiness makes us smile; joy makes us weep.

Happiness is obvious; joy is mysterious.

For one moment of joy, we would gladly exchange months of happiness. It breaks our heart, and we bleed. It squeezes our heart, and tears come out. It hollows out our heart and enlarges it.

The occasions for joy are as unpredictable and uncontrollable as joy itself. They can be totally undetectable—we can just "enter into joy"—or the cause can be very clear, like a recovery from the brink of death.

Of course, if you believe in God, you know where joy comes from and where it leads to and what it means. Where it comes from is God, and where it leads to is Heaven, and what it means is that God loves you so much that He wants you to share His joy, wants you in on the secret of why the Perfect Being never gets bored or boring.

The Good News is not just that God loves us but that He is crazy in love with us. *Us*, who are not only stupid and shallow and silly but morally insane (that is, immorally insane), who choose the fearful over the cheerful, the misery of selfishness over the joy of selflessness, despite our universal experience of the results of that experiment. God is not just proper and correct and philanthropic in His love. He is crazy. He is as super-rationally insane as we are sub-rationally insane. We are crazy-bad, but God is crazy-good. He is madly in love with His severely brain-and-heart-damaged children, and we cannot know the reason for that because that reason is not to be found in us but only in Him.

2. The Joy of the Longing for Joy

The longing for joy is not just a desire but a longing. The special German word for it is *Sehnsucht*. This very longing for joy is joy.

In his autobiography, *Surprised by Joy*, C. S. Lewis uses the word "joy" in a special sense, to mean the mysterious desire itself rather than its fulfillment. Here is how he defines it in *The Pilgrim's Regress*:

> The experience is one of intense longing. It is distinguished from other longings by two things. In the first place, though the sense of want is acute and even painful, yet the mere wanting is felt to be somehow a delight. Other desires are felt as pleasures only if satisfaction is expected in the near future: hunger is pleasant only while we know (or believe) that we are soon going to eat. But this desire, even when there is no hope of possible satisfaction, continues to be prized, and even to be preferred to anything else in the world, by those who have once felt it. This hunger is

better than any other fullness; this poverty better than all other wealth. . . .

In the second place, there is a peculiar mystery about the object of this Desire. . . . A far off hillside . . . some event in the past . . . "perilous seas and faerie lands forlorn" . . . erotic suggestions . . . magic and occultism . . . the intellectual craving for knowledge . . . I have myself been deluded by every one of these false answers in turn. . . . Every one of these supposed *objects* for the Desire is inadequate to it. . . .

It appeared to me therefore that if a man diligently followed this desire, pursuing the false objects until their falsity appeared and then resolutely abandoning them, he must come out at last into the clear knowledge that the human soul was made to enjoy some object that is never fully given —nay, cannot even be imagined as given—in our present mode of subjective and spatio-temporal experience. This Desire was, in the soul, as the Siege Perilous in Arthur's castle—the chair in which only one could sit. And if nature makes nothing in vain, the One who can sit in this chair must exist.[1]

That is Lewis' signature argument for the God and Heaven that can alone give us the joy that is the object of *Sehnsucht*. He puts the argument even more succinctly in *Mere Christianity*: "Creatures are not born with desires unless satisfaction for those desires exists. A baby feels hunger: well, there is such a thing as food. A duckling wants to swim: well, there is such a thing as water. Men feel sexual desire: well, there is such a thing as sex. If I find in myself a desire which

[1] C. S. Lewis, *The Pilgrim's Regress* (Grand Rapids, Mich.: Eerdmans, 2014), 234–37.

no experience in this world can satisfy, the most probable explanation is that I was made for another world."[2]

Here is one small example, out of many, from Lewis' fiction (from *The Voyage of the "Dawn Treader"*, one of the Chronicles of Narnia) about this mysterious longing. Lucy is exploring the Magician's Book:

> On the next page she came to a spell "for the refreshment of the spirit." The pictures were fewer here but very beautiful. And what Lucy found herself reading was more like a story than a spell. It went on for three pages and before she had read to the bottom of the page she had forgotten that she was reading at all. She was living in the story as if it were real, and all the pictures were real too. When she had got to the third page and come to the end, she said, "That is the loveliest story I've ever read or ever shall read in my whole life. Oh, I wish I could have gone on reading it for ten years. At least I'll read it over again."
>
> But here the magic of the Book came into play. You couldn't turn back. The right-hand pages, the ones ahead, could be turned; the left-hand pages could not.
>
> "Oh, what a shame!" said Lucy. "I did so want to read it again. Well, at least I must remember it. Let's see . . . it was about . . . about . . . oh dear, it's all fading away again. And even this last page is going blank. This is a very strange book. How can I have forgotten? It was about a cup and a sword and a tree and a green hill, I know that much. But I can't remember and what shall I do?"
>
> And she never could remember; and ever since that day what Lucy means by a good story is a story which reminds her of the forgotten story in the Magician's Book.[3]

[2] C. S. Lewis, *Mere Christianity* (1952; New York: HarperCollins, 2001), 136.

[3] C. S. Lewis, *The Voyage of the "Dawn Treader"* (New York: HarperCollins, 2001), 497.

Of course we are Lucy, and the Book is life, and the pages
are time, and the Magician is God, who gives us the appetizers of life-in-time (*bios*) to whet our appetites for His eternal life (*zōē*), which begins in time and is transplanted up
to eternity at death, as His divine life is transplanted down
from eternity into time in the Incarnation. But Lewis' story
is much more than an allegory, a puzzle to be solved; it's
an appetizer to be tasted, a music to be listened to, a range
of meanings to be teased with, wondered at, and delighted
in, but not captured. It's like a rainbow, not like a treasure
chest to which the rainbow points. The treasure chest is a
symbol and pointer to the rainbow, not vice versa.

When NASA sent *Voyager* I and II out of the solar system,
they added a recording of "The Sounds of Earth" for any extraterrestrials who might be out there. On it was Beethoven's
Opus 130. Beethoven had labeled it, in the margin, "Sehnsucht". The mysterious desire.

The Latin root of the word "desire" is *de sidere*, which
means "from the stars". Many things can provoke or cat-
alyze this joy, but they are only appetizers, signs, fingers that
point to the moon (or the stars), not the moon. (We are
fools most of the time, taking the finger for the moon, like a
dog who comes and sniffs your finger when you point to his
food.) For instance, this longing is experienced in the magic
words of the poets; or in the wordless words of great music,
work of the Muses, not just of man; or in the word spoken by human love, when one of the world's most prosaic
words suddenly becomes full of wonder and joy, the word
"we"; or in the solemn joy of high liturgy, the adoration of
the incredible mystery of God-with-us, when we are side by
side with Mary, hailed by the angelic annunciation of the
Heavenly glory; or when a great work of art becomes for
us no longer an object in this world but a window opening

up to another world, like the picture of *The Dawn Treader* to the Pevensie children; or in the electrical shock of the whole world being transformed overnight into something high, clear, and crystal by a perfect snowfall; or in the seagull's haunting, harking call to return to Mother Sea. Even if you have never known this heartbreaking joy in this world, you will know it in the next when you are swept up by your guardian angel into the golden chariot that Heaven's Prince has sent to fetch His Cinderella bride out of the cinders of this burning fireplace of a world to take you for a far, midnight ride to His very own castle and bedchamber where Glory will beget glory upon you forever.[4]

3. The Joy of Sex

Of all the things in this life that give us ecstatic appetizers of joy, sex is the most obvious and the most well known.

By "sex", I mean not just copulation but mental as well as physical orgasm, *ek-stasis*, "standing-outside yourself" in the total gift of yourself body and soul to the one person you solemnly pledge your all to (and therefore also your lifetime and your children). It is a mystical experience. It is increasingly rare in our cynical, anti-romantic, pragmatic, utilitarian, instrumentalist age. "Standing outside yourself" (in your consciousness) and "the total gift of yourself" (in your heart and will) sound logically self-contradictory. But it happens. In fact, it is, even today, the most common of all out-of-body experiences. And this out-of-body experience is also the most obviously bodily thing we do. And it brings us not only out of our bodies but also out of our minds.

[4] See my *Heaven: The Heart's Deepest Longing* (San Francisco: Ignatius Press, 1989), 233–34.

Animals experience sex only as pleasure. Humans enter into the next dimension, happiness, whenever sex is accompanied by personal love (which at least most people experience, though some pitiable people never do). Joy is the next dimension.

What does it mean? Sex seems to *mean* something more than itself. But not something like a code or an allegory or a moral lesson to figure out with the intellect, but something mystical, something that comes from the heart of the heart and that always evades and transcends us. Even on the happiness level, sex *means* something; but there, it means something obvious: it means "I love the one who loves me; I am loved by the one I love." On the joy level, it means more: something like "This is a pale copy of the ultimate secret of everything; this is an icon of the eternal Trinitarian life and love of God." Even if you do not believe that with your mind, you cannot help feeling something like that. Sex is a door in the walls of the world. When we open that door, we enter a holy place.

Much, much more has been said about this in our sex-obsessed age, much of it either nonsense or trivia, but some of it profoundly true and life-changing. I recommend Jay Budziszewski's *The Meaning of Sex*, Christopher Derrick's *Sex and Sacredness*, Patrick Coffin's *Sex au naturel*, and Saint John Paul II's "theology of the body", as expounded by Christopher West, especially in *Fill These Hearts* and *The Theology of the Body for Beginners*. Try it, you'll like it. A lot.

4. The Joy of Death

Death is also obviously a door through the walls of the world. It is the definitive door, the final door, the one-way door.

Sex and death have always been connected.

On the biological level, they are connected. Simple organisms like amoebas do not die until their host dies, if they are parasitic, like cancer cells, or until an external accident kills them. They do not have sex because they do not have death. Amoebas reproduce asexually, by fission. Higher organisms reproduce by sexual fusion. Sex is our way of outwitting death. To put the same point back-to-front, death is the price we pay for sex.

On the poetic level, sex and death are intuitively connected. The French call orgasm "la petite mort", "the little death". The connection is not culturally relative; it transcends culture, race, and religion.

On the mystical level, too, sex and death are connected. The consummation of human life and history, according to the last book of the Bible, is a spiritual marriage between God and man, the Lamb and His bride. The mystics of every religion use sexual analogies for the ecstasy of union with God. Every religion of the world tells the ego, the I, the very self, that it can live only if it gives itself away, dies to itself. C. S. Lewis says: "Die before you die; there is no chance after."[5] Augustine says: "Let me die, lest I die."[6] Even Nietzsche knew that the meaning of life was not the happiness of self-fulfillment but the ecstasy of "self-overcoming".

Literal death (death to the body) and spiritual death (death to the ego) are analogies of each other and give meaning to each other. If future technology abolishes physical death (by genetic engineering), it will also abolish religion (and, therefore, spiritual death or ecstasy), for all the religions of the world offer themselves as the only answer to death. The

[5] C. S. Lewis, *Till We Have Faces: A Myth Foretold* (1956; San Diego: Harcourt Brace, 1984), 279.

[6] Saint Augustine, *Confessions*, bk. 1, no. 5.

earliest human artefacts are religious and funerary. Technological (genetically engineered) immortality would also
abolish joy, hope, religion, eternity, mysticism, poetry, and
probably even more-than-animal sex. That would be literally
what C. S. Lewis calls "the abolition of man". It would be
the final triumph of "man's conquest of nature", which Fran-
cis Bacon and other early modern philosophers announced
as our culture's new *summum bonum*, or greatest good or
meaning of life on earth. It would be the final stage of "the
conquest of nature" because it would be the conquest of human nature. But it would not be Heaven on earth; it would
be Hell on earth. If you want to experience a hint or analogy of what it would feel like, leave a dozen eggs out on the
table for a year, then smell them. As C. S. Lewis says, "We
are like eggs at present. And you cannot go on indefinitely
being just an ordinary, decent egg. We must be hatched or
go bad."[7]

5. The Mystical Equation of Joy and Suffering

The joy of sex and the joy of death are both mystical, but
most people intuitively understand at least something about
them. The more difficult joy to understand is the joy of
suffering.

Let's try.

There is a mystical equation of suffering with joy. It is the
spiritual equivalent of the equation of matter with energy
(E equals M times C squared).

Energy is the border between the material and the spiritual. There are two kinds of energy, material and spiritual;
and as material energy is the physical side of the border be-

[7] Lewis, *Mere Christianity*, 199.

tween matter and spirit, spiritual energy is the spiritual side of that border. As there are two kinds of energy, material energy and spiritual energy, there are two kinds of suffering, material suffering and spiritual suffering.

In order to get to this mystical equation of suffering and joy, let's start with something about suffering that is much more common and easier to see. Let's look at the failed attempt to solve the problem of suffering with the simple logic of justice that we see in the speeches of Job's three friends: Job suffers, therefore he must have deserved to suffer. Now let's contrast that answer with the very different, much more mystical, answer of the author of the Book of Job, which he puts into the mouth of God at the end: "Where were you when I laid the foundations of the earth?" (Job 38:4). In other words, "I didn't notice you there when I designed the world's story. Did I miss something?"

The atheists' strongest argument against religion in general and Christianity in particular is the problem of suffering, the problem of why bad things happen to good people, the problem of the apparent contradiction between an all-good, all-powerful, and all-wise God and the existence of undeserved and apparently unnecessary suffering. For if God were all-good, He would will only our greatest good, our joy; and if God were all-powerful, He would get all that He wills; and if God were all-wise, He would know exactly what is best for us. And, therefore, if God existed, we would get only good and not evil. But we get evil as well as good: death as well as life, pain as well as pleasure, failure as well as success, suffering as well as joy. Even if some sufferings help us and strengthen us, many times our sufferings drive us to rebellion and despair. God may seem present in the first kind of suffering, but He seems horribly absent in the second. This, in lived rather than logical form, was the problem of Job on his dung heap. It was also the problem of Jesus on the Cross: "My God, my God, why have you forsaken me?" How can we trust a God who seems to let His children down so spectacularly?

The tempting answer is theodicy, the attempt by reason "to justify the ways of God to men", in Milton's famous phrase. The alcoholic poet's response to this claim is more palatable: that "malt does more than Milton can/ To justify God's ways to man."[8]

Job's three friends tried to do theodicy. Their intention may have been good (or it may have been bad: to condemn Job rather than to justify God), but the result was bad. It usually is. Why? Not because God is really irrational, but because *we* are, even at our best. We are stupid. We are not God. (Stop the presses!) And we are certainly not His defense attorneys, any more than we are His prosecuting attorneys. Both of those positions are existentially false, no matter how rationally sound the arguments we make from those positions may be. For their foundation, their *platform*, is false. Ed Muskie, a Maine Democrat who was campaigning for president in Iowa, climbed atop a manure spreader and told his farmer audience that this was the only time he had ever given a Democratic speech from a Republican platform.

God is not in the dock, for either the defense or the prosecution. We are.

That's the biblical answer. It's not more rational, nor is it less rational, than the arguments of theodicy; it's more existential, more accurate with respect to who we are.

And once this existential answer is given, the rational answer looks more reasonable: If there is indeed a God who

---

[8] A. E. Houseman, "A Shropshire Lad", in *Collected Poems* (London: Wordsworth Editions, 2005), 74.

is infinitely wiser than we are (and if there is not, then He does not deserve the name and we had better be atheists), He might very well allow apparently unreasonable and unnecessary and pointless sufferings to happen to us because He sees, as we do not, that they are reasonable and necessary and good for us in the end. "All things are good" is obviously nonsense, but "in everything God works for good" is not obviously nonsense. In other words, what is apparently true and what is really true may not be identical. Only to omniscience are appearance and reality identical. And it just might possibly be true that we do not have omniscience, that we are not God.

Even agnostic Socrates knew that: that only fools claim to be wise, and all the wise know they are fools. That was his Lesson One, and it is the intellectual equivalent of Jesus' moral Lesson One: that only sinners claim to be saints, and all the saints know they are sinners.

This answer to the problem of evil, which we could summarize in the two-word formula "existential humility", is not an excuse for not giving logical answers. It is not an alternative to rational answers. It does not deny the need for rational answers. It is not irrationalism or anti-intellectualism. It is an addition, not a subtraction. It puts a human frame around the logical answers. It is reasonable, for it is a reasonable consequence of what God said to Job and to Saint Catherine, in a vision, when He summarized everything He wanted to get across to us in the Bible in four syllables: "I'm God, you're not." (My favorite sermon in the world, partly because it's the shortest.)

That two-sentence summary of theism is either true or false. If it's false, then atheism is the true alternative to both of those two sentences: not only is God not God, but we are, for if there is no God, we are the highest being, the highest authority. But if God's little sermon is true, then it is not only true but fruitful; it explains all the data, like a good scientific hypothesis. It explains the data of our ignorance of God's plans. It explains why we cannot explain evil. For if we *did* understand "the mystery of evil", we would be as wise as God, and that would *refute* theism. That would make the characters in the play that we call human life to be equal to the Author of the play—which is just as atheistic as the denial that there is any Author.

But all this, though necessary, is not sufficient. It is only a negative answer, a defensive answer. It merely pulls the claws from the atheistic lion, the stinger from the atheistic bee. It does not prove the theistic hypothesis; it just disproves its disproof. It leaves the debate in a stalemate. We need more.

What we need are not necessarily proofs. Do we have or need *proof* that the physical world is not a hypnotic dream from a powerful evil spirit or that our parents are not very well-disguised aliens? What we need are merely *good reasons*. These are not primarily syllogisms but intuitions, insights, understandings, "big pictures", shafts of light that partly pierce the gloom of seeing "through a glass, darkly". As Pascal said, God gives us just enough light to see by, so that seekers find and non-seekers do not. This is neither too little light, so that even seekers do not find, nor too much light, so that even non-seekers find, against their will, as we find the blinding light of the sun at midday. For in that case, we would have no freedom of choice, and the heart would have no role to play, only the head and the eyes. We do not *choose* to believe in the light of the noonday sun, but Juliet does choose to believe in Romeo's love.

So our faith cannot be proved, but it cannot be disproved, and it can be shown to be reasonable. Since we are in a story, a play, or a novel, and not yet at the end of it, our present sufferings may well be necessary birth pangs that we will eventually look back on with acceptance and even gratitude. Saint Teresa, who suffered greatly, said that the most painful life on earth, looked back on from the perspective of Heaven, will seem no more than one night in an inconvenient hotel. That truth cannot be proved, of course, but it is reasonable. And it is consistent with many little clues in this life, little foretastes of Heaven that come only after Purgatorial sufferings, like childbirth, or the Chicago Cubs finally winning the World Series after over a century of frustration. In fact, it is true of every good story. If the story went straight from "once upon a time" to "they all lived happily ever after", it would not be a story at all.

All this is a traditional and unoriginal answer to the atheist's strongest argument, the problem of evil. But there is more. If we look more carefully at joy, at sorrow, and at the relation between them, we can see that they need each other, imply each other, and are the cause of each other and also the effect of each other. They are in a mystical equation. They are two sides of the same coin, the coin of any human life that is truly happy, truly blessed, truly perfect and complete.

This is true for two reasons. One is obvious and well known, the other is not. The obvious one is the psychological truism that our suffering increases our joy because we appreciate opposites only by contrast. (Whether this was so before the Fall or not, I do not know. Presumably, it will not be true in Heaven. Or, if it is, then there will be blessed suffering in Heaven, too, but there we will fully understand and accept and love its blessings.)[9]

---

[9] Why do we always use spatial language for Heaven ("there") instead of temporal language ("then")? What if Heaven is not a different place, or a different kind of place, within our life's time, but a different time, or a

But the second reason is more mystical: not just a causal dependence but an *equation* between suffering and joy.

It is analogous to the famous Einsteinian equation of matter with energy. The physical equation is that energy equals matter multiplied by the square of the absolute in material physics, the speed of light; and the mystical equation is that joy equals suffering multiplied by the Cross of the absolute in mystical physics, which is Jesus Christ, "the light of the world". He unifies joy and suffering as light unifies matter and energy.

We can see this mystical equation of joy and suffering in all the events of Christ's life, culminating in His Passion and death, which are neither an accident nor a postscript, appendix, or addition, but the very consummation, the fruit and flower, of His life. He lived backward, for he lived in order to die; and we can understand His life only if we follow his life with our thought and think backward, as we can understand a rose only if we look backward from the flower to the plant.

To understand the meaning of life, we must look at Christ, for Christ not only reveals God to man, but "fully reveals man to man himself".[10] This was the favorite quote of Pope Saint John Paul II from the documents of Vatican II. It was also the final point of the greatest work of Christian apologetics since Saint Thomas Aquinas, namely, Pascal's *Pensées*: "Apart from Jesus Christ we cannot know the meaning of our life or our death, of God, or of ourselves."[11] What else is there than that?

---

different kind of time, within our life's place, which is "the heavens and the earth," i.e., this universe? See Mark Helprin's vision on page 44.

[10] *Pastoral Constitution on the Church in the Modern World Gaudium et Spes* (December 7, 1965), no. 22.

[11] Blaise Pascal, *Pensées*, trans. A. J. Krailsheimer, rev. ed. (London: Penguin Books, 1995), 121.

Just as we can formulate the physical equation between matter and energy as E equals M times C squared, we can formulate the mystical equation of joy and suffering symbolically as J equals S times C squared, J being joy, S being suffering, and C being Christ. (There is even a kind of pun in the two equations: they use the same "C", just as "God's Son" and "God's sun" use the same sound. Also, this "C" is an immense mystical *sea*. God is not above making puns.)

Christ is the absolute, the spiritual constant, the speed of divine light made visible to man in man. As physical light unifies apparently irreconcilable physical opposites, both in the universe (it alone unifies matter and energy) and in itself (it alone is both undulatory and corpuscular, both wave and particle, both continuous and discrete), so Christ unifies apparently irreconcilable opposites: infinite God and finite man, invisible spirit and visible matter, the "yes" of joy and the "no" of suffering. (And also justice and mercy.)

And just as it is not simply C but C squared that unites matter and energy in Einstein's equation, so it is not simply Christ that unites joy and suffering but Christ squared, Christ multiplied by Himself. How does He multiply Himself? In His Body, by giving up His Body, in three ways: on the Cross, in the Church (all those little Christs), and in the Eucharist. "The Body of Christ" is one in those three places and forms. In all three, He squares Himself, He multiplies Himself, He gives Himself to all of us.

The Eucharist is the summit, the sum, and the substance of life for the Christian who knows it as Christ Himself. But the Eucharist celebrates and re-presents not only Christ's Resurrection but also His death; not only His supreme joy but also His supreme suffering, by the *separation* of the Body and the Blood.

There are more parallels. Just as Einstein's equation was the principle behind the unleashing of the greatest energy in matter, the energy that binds the atom together, when the unsplittable was split ("atom" means, literally, "unsplittable"); so the mystical equation was the principle behind the unleashing of the energy of salvation, the energy of divine love, when the unsplittable atom of the Trinity was split in the only way it could be: subjectively, not objectively; psychologically, not ontologically; when the Son was forsaken by the Father. What happened on Calvary was the second Big Bang. The first one, 13.7 billion years ago, unleashed all the power in the universe; the second one, 2000 years ago, unleashed all the love in the Trinity.

There were two Big Bangs, not just one. First, 13.7 billion years ago God made being out of non-being; then, 2000 years ago He made Heaven out of Hell. The second Bang was greater than the first because Hell is even worse than non-being. (That's why Christ said about Judas that "it would have been better for that man if he had never been born.")

When Christians pray the Stations of the Cross, they address the dying Christ with the Greek words *Hagios ho Theos, hagios Ischyros, hagios Athanatos, eleison hūmas* ("Holy God, holy strong One, holy immortal One, have mercy on us"). We call the One who died "the Immortal One", the one who *cannot* die.

A paradox is an apparent contradiction. A contradiction is simply impossible: X cannot be non-X. There are no real contradictions. But there are paradoxes, or apparent contradictions. They are of two kinds. Most of them can be resolved by distinguishing two senses or aspects: in one sense, yes; in another sense, no; thus both yes and no. (But it cannot be both yes and no in the very same sense, for that would be meaningless, that would be simply X, which is X, being not X.) The second kind of paradox cannot be thus unraveled by reason making a distinction between two senses, at least not in this life. Perhaps Christ is the only such paradox; perhaps there are others. I don't know.

Let's see how this mystical equation casts new light on other mysteries of the faith.

Let's apply it to the mysteries of the Rosary. For the Rosary is really the Gospel. It's not just a Catholic thing but a Catholic meditation on the essential Christian thing. Its fifteen traditional mysteries are the essential biblical events of our salvation.

Each of the five Joyful Mysteries implicitly includes suffering and sorrow, and each of the five Sorrowful Mysteries implicitly includes joy.

By the way, why are there *five* mysteries of each kind? Perhaps because there are five wounds in the dying Christ's body, as there are five points to a star. Only points pierce and hurt. The Hindu and Buddhist image of the wheel, or the circle, has no points. The image of the Cross has points: four of them. So does the image of the Trinity, the triangle, have points. So does the image of the six-pointed Star of David.

The first Joyful Mystery, the Annunciation, was God's invitation to Mary to consent freely to give birth to the Man of Sorrows and to share those sorrows as no other creature ever did. (Read Luke 2:35, and then contemplate the Pietà for half an hour. I dare you.) This is life's greatest sorrow even on a human level: a mother's sorrow for her dead son. When His sacred heart was pierced with the centurion's lance, her immaculate heart was pierced, too. In fact, she would gladly have exchanged places with Him. On a human level, she may have suffered more than He did, because love suffers more in the beloved's sufferings than in its own, since love multiplies both joys and sufferings by the quantity of its love, and love (*agapē*) loves the beloved more than itself.

Her "fiat", her Yes in the Annunciation, was a Yes to the whole deal, the whole equation, the unimaginable sorrow and the unimaginable joy, unimaginably and inextricably intertwined.

The second Joyful Mystery, the Visitation, was the occasion for the mutual greeting of the two greatest martyrs, Jesus and John the Baptist, whom Jesus called the greatest of all the prophets (Mt 11:11), when both were in their mothers' wombs. Soon John's body would lose its head and Jesus' body would lose its blood.

Even Mary's joyful *Magnificat*, sung on this joyful occasion, includes "the dark side", for its subject is spiritual warfare. It praises the God who humbles the exalted as well as exalting the humble, who empties the rich as well as filling the poor.

The third Joyful Mystery, the Nativity, was Christ's entrance into this world of sin, suffering, and death—like a spy parachuting into enemy territory. He came to fight. In fact, He came to die. He was the only man who came into this world, not to live, but to die. And Mary was His means to that end. She was His landing field. Yes, the Incarnation was love, but it was also war. And war always has casualties.

In the fourth Joyful Mystery, the Presentation in the Temple, Mary gave her son up to that end: to war, to death, and to us. It was like Abraham offering up Isaac on Mount Moriah (which according to tradition was later called Mount Zion and was where the Temple stood), and it was like God the Father offering up His own Son on Calvary (which was on that same Mount Zion). And we call this a "joyful" mystery!

The fifth Joyful Mystery, the Finding of the Christ Child

in the Temple, was like a death and resurrection to Mary. This loss was the only way the immaculate one could share the grief of us sinners, for she could not lose Jesus spiritually. But she lost Him physically for three days when He was twelve, and later, for three days, between His death and Resurrection, when He was thirty-three. Is there any greater sorrow in life than a mother's loss of her child?

So all five Joyful Mysteries bespeak sorrows. The five Sorrowful Mysteries, on the other hand, all bespeak joys.

The Agony in the Garden, like the temptations in the wilderness three years earlier, was a victory, for it was Christ's conquest of Satan, not Satan's conquest of Christ. The Son of God had assumed a fleshly weakness by His Incarnation as the Son of Man. This weakness was his Achilles' heel (the Achilles myth is an uncanny insight into the same truth as Genesis 3:15); and that heel was now being bruised as severely as anything human could possibly be. But only for a time, so that Satan's head could be not just bruised but beaten into the dust forever by Christ, "who for the *joy* that was set before him endured the cross, despising the shame" (Heb 12:2; emphasis added). Temptation is not a joy, but overcoming temptation is.

The Scourging at the Pillar was His love and kindness accepting all the cruelty and hatred of the world and draining it off, emptying it out like a blotter. It was thus the triumph of love over hate, though it seemed to be the triumph of hate over love. And since love is the greatest joy and hate is the greatest misery, it was the triumph of joy over misery.

The Crowning with Thorns was not only a crowning with *thorns*, but also a *crowning*. It transformed thorns into diamonds. It was the triumph of true kingship: the kingship not of power, but of love.

The Carrying of the Cross was a holy Exchange. His

Cross, which He did not deserve, relieved us of our cross, which we did deserve. That is the Good News. And our task now, like that of Simon of Cyrene, is to take up His Cross— and that is part of the Good News, too: that our sufferings can now be participations in His, because our taking up our cross is now our taking up *His* Cross. Christ did something far better and more joyful than removing our sufferings: He transformed them. They can now be part of His redemption. And that redemption is joy for both Him and us. As the pain was part of His joy, our pain can be part of our joy if we are "in" Him.

The Crucifixion was the greatest evil that ever happened, the torture and murder of God. But it was also the greatest good that ever happened: our salvation. We do not call it "Bad Friday" or "Black Friday" but "Good Friday". If He can turn even this greatest of evils into the greatest of goods, He can do the same to everything: "Behold, I make all things new."

The point of this mystical equation of joy and suffering is not that suffering is no longer suffering but that we can find joy in it because God has inserted Himself into it. Infinite Joy has united Himself with our sufferings so that we can unite our sufferings with His joy. Because Christ has joined suffering and joy, we can find Him, and therefore find Infinite Love, and therefore the infinite joy that necessarily follows from infinite love, even at the heart of suffering.

Of course this "works" only if we love Him and trust Him. "In everything [even evil things] God works for good *with those who love him."* That's the "catch": that we must choose to leap into the river of His mysterious grace, into his arms; that the astonishing blessing of all things working together for good for us depends on our free choice to love Him and to trust Him—that's the catch. But it's surely very strange to describe either love or trust or free choice as a "catch".

These events in Christ's life are called "mysteries", not because they lack light, but because they have inexhaustible depth due to their very excess of light. There is a spillover, an excess. Our containers cannot contain them. That is why, when Eternity touches time, time trembles, like a woman being impregnated. And that is why we weep when our heart feels either a sorrow or a joy that it cannot contain. That is also why Jesus wept (Jn 11:35, the shortest verse in the Bible). Jesus is God's tears. That's "*good* news."

Even outside Christianity, on a secular level, suffering and love, and therefore suffering and joy, are psychologically joined. Even wise atheists know that sacrifice is the surest and highest expression of love. When Jesus extended His nail-pierced hands on the Cross, He was saying: "See, this is how much I love you." So it is love that is the constant in the mystical equation that joins suffering and joy. Christ is that constant, because Christ is God and God is love (*agapē*).

And even if one does not believe in divine love, one can believe in human love. Even if the unbeliever denies that human love goes all the way up to the divine in Christ, he can believe that Christ comes all the way down to human love.

Suffering and love multiply their power when they work together. Suffering without love accomplishes little in the end because whatever is loveless is joyless and brittle and angry. Love without suffering also accomplishes little in the end because it is easy and thin and shallow and sentimental. The power to "make all things new" is found neither in the Cross without Christ nor in Christ without the Cross; neither in the terrorists' hard perversions of Islam nor in the

100 Doors in the Walls of the World

modernists' soft perversions of Christianity; neither in suffering without love nor in love without suffering; but only
in the fruitful union of both. Suffering love is the greatest
power in the universe. Sufi Muslims and Hasidic Jews and
Bhakti Hindus and Pure Land Buddhists know that too, but
only Christians also know *why* it works and how it accom-
plished the defeat of the Devil and our eternal salvation,
because this "it" is really a "who".

We find some version of this mystical equation at the
heart of every religion. It is the secret of life-coming-from-
death spiritually, even if it is not clear to all religions that
it also happens physically, by a final resurrection. It is the
paradox of a self being called to unselfishness, the secret
of self-fulfillment-by-self-emptying, of victory-by-surrender-
to-God. It is at the very heart of Islam, for the very word "islam" means "surrender" or "the peace (*shalom*) that comes
through surrender". It is at the heart of Taoism, where it is
called *wei wu wei*, "doing by not doing", or active passivity.
It is Gandhi's "nonviolent resistance". Its apparent weakness is its supreme power, because when your ego gets off
the throne of your life, God takes its place, and the result
is Power and Life and Resurrection and Salvation and Joy.

Suffering accepted can mean the very same thing as love.
Both can mean the ego getting off the throne; both can mean
"not my will but Thine be done." For what is suffering but
the contradiction between my will (i.e., my desires) and my
satisfactions? When I substitute God's will for mine, con-
sciously (in Western religions) or even unconsciously (in
Eastern religions), I put to death the "my" of my will; I
renounce my sovereignty. I embrace "*not* my will be done"
instead of "my will be done." I embrace the essence of suffering. And, as Buddha discovered, this "nirvana" or "ex-
tinction" of self-will, which seems to be the entering into

suffering, is really the entering into "bliss" or joy. Because one of the two forces that are necessary for suffering, my willed refusal of it, is gone.

When suffering is embraced with love, "not my will be done" becomes my will. That is the paradox of finding yourself (and your joy) by losing yourself (and your demand for joy). Buddha failed to see that the power here is not just in the negative half, that is, the "not my will be done", but above all in the positive half, the "Your will be done, because I love You and I trust Your love for me." Love makes sacrifice and its sufferings into the opposite of suffering, joy. To put the same paradox in other words, what you suffer in love is not misery but joy. That's right: you *suffer* joy. Unlike happiness, joy is a suffering, a surprise, a being-ravished, a kind of spiritual orgasm. It tears you apart! The source of your joy comes not from inside you but from outside you; it comes, not from your plans and desires and will for the future, but it comes creeping up on you from behind, or from the side, from your self-forgetfulness. By far the most powerful way to this self-forgetfulness is not the Buddhist way, which lacks a divine lover, but the Christian way, where it comes from the self-forgetfulness in your love of the Heavenly beloved. (It can also come to an unbeliever anonymously, from the self-forgetfulness in the love of the earthly beloved.) This is why we must suffer: so that we give up the doomed project of finding joy by our own efforts, our own desires. It never works. The deepest problems are ones we cannot solve by *doing* anything about them! You can't make yourself pregnant.

There are only two roads to joy, and one simply doesn't get there while the other does. What reason seems to contradict, experience proves: the mystical, paradoxical way works while the obvious, non-paradoxical way does not.

This mystical way, the mystical equation of joy and suffering, is a way, not for a few mystics, but for everyone. And
it's not an optional way; it's the only way to joy. Only when
God answers the prayer of John Donne, "Batter my heart,
three-person'd God";[12] only when T. S. Eliot's "wounded
surgeon plies the steel"[13] do we receive the heart transplant
that we need in order to experience Heavenly joy.

Salvation is a heart transplant operation. That's why we
have to die. Death is like anesthesia. Before death the pa-
tient hops around on the operating table telling the Surgeon
what to do. Death is God's gentle way of saying, "Sleep now,
my little child", or—same thing in other words—"Quiet,
fool!"

Salvation is a blood transfusion. For, as Scripture says,
"without the shedding of blood there is no forgiveness of
sins" (Heb 9:22), for "the life of the flesh is in the blood"
(Lev 17:11). And Christ's Blood, Christ's life, is transplanted
into the veins of our souls in the sacraments. It is His literal
Blood in the Eucharist, but it is the same divine life (*zōē*) in
the other sacraments. Christ is the anti-Dracula, and Dracula is the Antichrist. Dracula, like Satan, sucks our blood,
our life, to make us one of the damned, the "living dead";
while Christ gives us His Blood, His life, to make us one of
the saved, the blessed dead who have died in the Lord and
therefore live. The Cross is the syringe that dispenses the
Precious Blood. The Cross is also like a scalpel or a sword.
It even *looks* like a sword, held at the hilt by the hand of
Heaven and plunged into us, not to take life, but to give
it. And we are privileged to consent to that operation and,

---

[12] John Donne, sonnet no. 14, in *Holy Sonnets* (Newton, N.J.: Vicarage
Hill Press, 2014), 30.
[13] T. S. Eliot, "East Coker", in *Four Quartets* (Boston: Mariner Books;
Houghton Mifflin, 1971), 29.

even more, to participate in it actively. To suffer and to die can be an *action*.

As blood spills from the hymen ("hymen" means "life") when the gift of new life is made possible through first sexual intercourse, so our blood must spill from our heart when we freely receive His life-giving thrust into our impregnated souls. Sex is an image of "the spiritual marriage". That is why it is a holy icon, not a casual entertainment. And that is why God must always be "He" to us, not "She". And that is also why contraception is sacrilegious.

If sex is like death, death is like sex. It is the fire of divine love. And therefore we need not fear it. For even if we disappear, even if the soul were not by nature immortal, still the God whose love called us forth out of nothing by creation will not cease to love us and will call us forth again. Once, out of the abyss of holy fire, out of the Burning Bush of His essential self, He spoke my name, the holy letter "I". Therefore I fear not to pick up my self into my hands and place it into His hands and leave it there upon His altar-forge (for love is a fire), where He will weld the broken shards of my poor self into a glorious sword, which in His fiery hands will swing and sing and cleave the air again.

I will therefore do with my soul, my only soul, what Abram did with Isaac, his only son, and what God Himself did with His Son, His only Son.

V

The Style: Art

1. Art's Importance

Beauty is a dimension of human life that transcends animal consciousness as absolutely as do our knowledge by theoretical reason of abstract eternal truth and our awareness by practical reason or conscience of obligatory moral goodness. Thus, beauty is one of the three largest doors in the walls of the world.

"Beauty will save the world", as Dostoyevsky said,[1] because beauty is what attracts us to believe in the truth and to choose the good. Beauty is what we fall in love with, and therefore beauty is our soul's gravity. As Augustine says, "pondus meum amor meus"[2]—my love is my weight, my gravity.

Art is not the cultivation of cleverness or ugliness or fashionableness. Neither is it the cultivation of prettiness. It is the cultivation of beauty.

The artistic style of a story is not an extraneous and accidental addition from outside, just as liturgy is not an extraneous addition to worship or the prettification of worship. Liturgy is worship. It is a dimension of all religion, just as

[1] Fyodor Dostoyevsky, *The Idiot*, trans. David McDuff (London and New York: Penguin Classics, 2004), 446.
[2] Saint Augustine, *Confessions* 13.9.10.

much as creeds and codes, theologies and moralities. It is not the wrapping; it is the present.

Christianity, unlike most other religions, is fundamentally a story, a piece of news, "the good news", or "gospel"; and the "style" of the book that tells this "good news", the New Testament, especially its four "Gospels", is also not wrapping. It is not a literary style; it is a personal "style". John describes Christ as "full of grace and truth" (Jn 1:18). The grace is not in the telling but in the One told. It is the "style" of Christ's humanity, not the style of the apostles' writing. The style of the writing, of the telling of the story, in the Gospels is not as artistic as the style of Cicero or Augustine; it is common or koine Greek. But no story ever had a more perfect "style" in the doing.

Narrative art has two dimensions: the story itself (what happened and what it means) and its telling (the words). In the Gospels, the story is the essence. Mark's and Matthew's style is not as beautiful as Luke's or John's, but their story is equally beautiful because it is the same story. It is *Jesus'* "style" that is the point. (Thus Jesus' unforgettable words in Matthew's Gospel contrast strikingly with Matthew's forgettable words. Matthew himself could never have spoken the Sermon on the Mount.)

2. Art's Highest Purpose

The importance of art can best be seen in looking at its highest purpose: that purpose is to break our hearts. For the only whole heart is the heart that has been broken.

Therefore, the highest praise we can give a human artist is what C. S. Lewis says:

Have you not seen that in our days,
Of any whose story, song, or art
Delights us, our sincerest praise
Means, when all's said, "You break my heart"?[3]

This obviously has something to do with our previous point, the joy of suffering. It assumes our heart's deep need to be broken. We all know, deep down, that the only whole heart is one that has been broken, although usually we do not understand why. It is not merely that it teaches us something, though that is true, too, as Rabbi Abraham Joshua Heschel says: "The man who has not suffered—what could he possibly know, anyway?" More, this breaking of hearts is a suffering that we treasure as a joy. In life, the joy comes later than the tears; in art, the joy comes at the same time as the tears. The tears of joy and the tears of suffering flow together when we discover a work of art that breaks our heart, like the end of *The Lord of the Rings*:

> And when the glad shout had swelled up and died away again, to Sam's final and complete satisfaction and pure joy, a minstrel of Gondor stood forth, and knelt, and begged leave to sing. And behold! he said: ". . . I will sing to you of Frodo of the Nine Fingers and the Ring of Doom."
>
> And when Sam heard that he laughed aloud for sheer delight, and he stood up and cried: "O great glory and splendour! And all my wishes have come true!" And then he wept.
>
> And all the host laughed and wept, and in the midst of their merriment and tears the clear voice of the minstrel rose like silver and gold, and all men were hushed. And he sang to them, now in the Elven-tongue, now in the speech of the West, until their hearts, wounded with sweet words, overflowed, and their joy was like swords, and they passed

---

[3] C. S. Lewis, *Poems* (New York: HarperOne, 2017), 203.

in thought out to regions where pain and delight flow together and tears are the very wine of blessedness.[4]

In his essay "On Fairy-Stories", Tolkien calls this the "eucatastrophe" (the "good catastrophe"):

> . . . when that sudden turn comes we get a piercing glimpse of joy or heart's desire: of heart's mending, of joy that can only come after the pain—that seems for a moment to pass outside the frame, to rend indeed the very web of story and let a gleam come through:
> "Seven long years I served for thee,
> The glassy hill I clamb for thee,
> The bluidy shirt I wrang for thee,
> And wilt thou not waken and turn to me?"
> He heard and turned to her.[5]

Eucatastrophe is the form that the art of breaking hearts takes in the genre of narrative. It happens in fiction because it happens in real life. We understand it much better in art than in life. That is why art is so educative to life. And that is why great novels are much more effective than any books of theory in making us good psychologists, good counselors, or even good friends.

We could call the art of breaking hearts "artbreak". This art is like breaking the chrysalis to release the butterfly. It gives our hearts wings to fly—to fly out of our bodies (great art gives us an out-of-body experience, an *ek-stasis*) and even out of this world. Our bodies stay behind on earth, while our spirits soar through this door in the wall into the outer courts of Heaven.

[4] J. R. R. Tolkien, *Lord of the Rings* (New York: Mariner Books; Houghton Mifflin, 2005), 954.

[5] J. R. R. Tolkien, *Tolkien on Fairy-Stories*, ed. Verlyn Flieger and Douglas A. Anderson (London: HarperCollins, 2008), 244.

There is a hierarchy of the arts. The two arts that have the most power to break hearts are music and storytelling. But visual arts can do it, too, especially architecture. The first time I ever saw a cathedral from inside, my heart would not let me breathe for at least five seconds.

The tears of artbreak water the growth of the plant of new life. It is Heavenly rain in our desert. Pity the poor person who has never been suddenly struck by its lightning and thunder.

Artbreak is not just a thrill, to relieve the boredom. It is necessary. It gives our heart the empty places into which God can pour Himself. It is Heavenly sculpting, Heavenly surgery.

Great art is quintessentially earthly and earthy, and at the same time is "inspired" or "in-breathed" by Heaven. For man alone blends earth and Heaven, as the only earthly part of Heaven and the only Heavenly part of earth, as the only spirit that is an animal and the only animal that is a spirit. We are amphibians.

Because we are amphibians, there are three kinds of art: arts of the beach, arts of the land, and arts of the sea; or human arts, natural arts, and divine arts. A few words about each in terms of its function in opening the doors in the wall:

3. Human Arts: Poetry, Music, Architecture

Human arts like poetry, music, architecture, and storytelling (of course there are many more) are not just arts *in* life, or arts that are parts of life, but arts that life *is*. All life is poetry (though many live it as if it were prose), all life is music (though many live noise instead), all life is architecture (we are constantly constructing the temple of ourselves).

Take poetry first. Real poetry, I mean; the poetry that has

moved hearts, not just tickled minds or relieved boredom. Such poetry is classic and immortal. Little or no contemporary poetry is immortal because it is typically written in a kind of semi-private code, created by and for a tiny, arrogant, self-referential, elitist in-group, a mutual admiration society. It is certainly not written for ordinary people. They cannot even understand it, much less wonder at it.

But poetry used to be public and popular. Greek, Roman, Persian, and Icelandic epics were written in poetry and chanted aloud. Everyone was familiar with them. For poetry is more ancient than prose. Poetic speech is prior to prosaic speech, both collectively and individually. Poetry is not later, ornamented prose; prose is later, de-poeticized poetry. Most children, primitives, and peasants are poets; most scholars, sophisticates, psychologists, scientists, politicians, and businesspersons are not.

Even within traditional poetry, only one line in a million breaks your heart and draws out blood and water. And such lines often occur in minor poems by minor poets. But when they do occur, they are unforgettable—like "a rose-red city —half as old as time",[6] or "the wrinkled sea beneath him crawls",[7] or "There is a Lady sweet and kind, / Was never face so pleased my mind; / I did but see her passing by, / And yet I love her till I die",[8] or "Born of the sun, they travelled a short while toward the sun / And left the vivid air singed with their honour."[9]

---

[6] John William Burgon, *Petra, a Prize Poem, Recited in the Theatre, Oxford, June IV, MDCCCXLV* (Charleston, S.C.: BiblioBazaar, 2009), 14.

[7] Alfred Lord Tennyson, "The Eagle", *Poems* (New York: Knopf, 2004), 43.

[8] Thomas Ford, "There Is a Lady Sweet and Kind", from *Music of Sundry Kinds* (1607), no. 70 in *The Oxford Book of English Verse, 1250–1900*, ed. Arthur Thomas Quiller-Couch (Oxford: Clarendon Press, 1912).

[9] Stephen Spender, "I think continually of those who were truly great", in *New Collected Poems* (London: Faber & Faber, 2004), XXIII.

Hamlet contains more such unforgettable lines and has more entries in *Bartlett's Familiar Quotations* than any other book but the Bible. Books of "prose" can also be utterly poetic, like Augustine's *Confessions*. For example, "Thou didst touch me, and I have burned for Thy peace",[10] or "Thou hast made us for Thyself and our hearts are restless till they rest in Thee."[11]

Such lines are not powerful because they are familiar; they are familiar because they are powerful. Like the canon of great books, there is a canon of great lines. Both canons are largely personal and subjective, but not wholly. Stupid, sappy lines like "Love means never having to say you're sorry"[12] never burned themselves into a human soul like "We must love one another or die."[13]

The effect such lines can have on receptive souls transcends their human causes. They are "inspired", that is, "in-breathed". Our minds are like stuffy rooms or caves, and such lines are breaths of fresh air from another world. We were living in Plato's Cave, and then we met Socrates. Where did he come from? Unlike all other philosophers, he did not come from previous philosophers. He was commissioned and commandeered by a god: the god of the Delphic oracle and the god of his personal *daimon*. Nietzsche is also inspired, from an opposite direction. There are doors in the floor of Plato's Cave as well as in the walls. *Zarathustra* was written semi-unconsciously, almost by "automatic writing". The power of its rhetoric is not just clever, it is from another dimension. Not all that is supernatural is good.

[10] Saint Augustine, *Confessions*, trans. F. J. Sheed, 2nd ed. (Indianapolis and Cambridge: Hackett, 2006), 10.27, p. 210.

[11] Ibid., 1.1, p. 3.

[12] Eric Segal, *Love Story* (New York: HarperTorch, 2012), 131.

[13] W. H. Auden, "September 1, 1939", in *Selected Poems* (New York: Vintage; Random House, 2007), 97.

Sometimes it is not just a single line but a whole play or a whole epic that has the power to break your heart. The obvious example here is *The Lord of the Rings* (and, for many, *The Silmarillion*) but it also applies to short works like *Our Town* (for everyone *except* the jaded teenagers who have to read it and sneer at it in high school); it broke the hearts of even the hard-hearted, money-grubbing Hollywood elites who wept when they first saw it. Movies, too, can have that power to stun and silence our popcorn. The obvious example is *The Passion of the Christ*, but that one depends largely on what you bring to it. The only other three movies that I have seen audiences weep over are *The Prisoner* (with Alec Guinness), *The Shawshank Redemption*, and *Dead Man Walking*. (All three, surprisingly, were prison movies; and in a sense so was *The Passion of the Christ*.)

The power to pierce our walls is even more widely felt and acknowledged in music. And what applies to music also applies to poetry because poetry is verbal music. A very small percentage of music seems to be not from this world, or at least not from this era. It sounds like a series of distant echoes from the music sung in the Garden of Eden. (Did this music come down to us through Jung's "collective unconscious"?) Charles Williams writes: "A voice went out from Eden. All great music was the fallen echo of that voice." Much of Chopin's music, for instance, sounds from that other dimension.

The first time I heard Beethoven's Ninth Symphony, alone in my room as a teenager, I felt a terror I had never felt before when the fourth movement burst into the choral ode: I thought I could never get back into my body again since I had become that music. Ordinary music, even very good music, does not have that power. It is a different kind of thing altogether.

When I first heard Palestrina's music, I knew without a

doubt that no man could have invented that music, but only angels. I was being given a preview of Heaven.

The small canon of such rare pieces of music exists, but it is very relative and variable, since we all have different ears in our hearts. For what we hear is not just the music but the otherwise-inexpressible mystical meaning that is carried to our hearts by the sound, whether it comes through chant or symphony, country western or opera, Beatles or Bach. I personally know three men, two philosophers and one monk, who were atheists or agnostics when they were younger and were converted by the music of Bach. They all, independently, said to me that what they intuitively heard in Bach was the Voice of God. (Karl Barth said the same about Mozart.) They all said, "There is the music of Bach; therefore, there must be a God." It was not arguable; it was immediately evident.

Jean Sibelius said that when he constructed a symphony he had the sense that God threw down the sounds from Heaven, like pieces of an enormous broken stained-glass window, and he had to try to reassemble them.

Nearly all great writers and musicians have said that the process of composing their greatest works was not *creation* but *discovery*. What they gave us in their poetry or their music or their stories did not originate with them. It was already there, eternally there. All these artists did was point to it, lift the curtain a few inches for a little while, the curtain that until then had hidden these things from our eyes. Wordsworth, Coleridge, Tolkien, T. S. Eliot, Paul Valery, and many more say this explicitly.

The literary critic or music critic is tempted merely to look *at* the work, but the reader or listener whose heart has been broken by it has looked *along* it. Think of two people in the Cave: one notices that there are windows in the walls and merely looks *at* them, as features of the Cave. The other looks *through* them at what is outside the Cave. It is not *in* the words or the music that we find the thing that breaks our hearts, but only *through* them.

If you say that this thing is God, I do not disagree with you. But I think that it is misleading to speak that way— as if, coming to the art with a mind full of an already determinate concept of God, we merely use our concept of God to interpret the art. That's OK, but the *spell* works the other way round: when the art interprets the theology rather than the theology interpreting the art. The art (only great art is meant here) supplies new content to the word "God". (Few things can be more precious than that!) God is now seen anew, as the One who inspired that unique work of art, rather than that unique work of art being seen merely as one of the many things inspired by the God we already knew. We don't find unsurprising divine fingerprints on the art; we find surprising artistic fingers on God.

Architecture is, in one way, the closest approach of any human art to the divine art of creating a universe. The cathedral of Notre Dame is a whole universe. (Just ask Quasimodo.) Architecture also bridges the distinction between civilization, which is visible (roads, armies, money, government, practical arts), and culture, which is invisible (values, sensibilities, beauties, religion, fine arts).

Cathedrals are miracles. They are not heavy material things in this world, but light angels from Heaven. Every time I see a picture of Notre Dame cathedral I am amazed that it has not blasted off to Heaven but is still on its landing pad. It even *looks* like a rocket; the flying buttresses are like rocket fins. One day Parisians will be surprised to find it suddenly gone. I won't.

Great pictures, too, are not just things in the world, enclosed things. They are also windows that open. We are invited to look through them, not at them. Some stories are like that, too, like George MacDonald's "The Golden Key", Tolkien's favorite fairy tale and mine, too.

4. *Natural Arts*

God is a better *everything* than we are; therefore, He is also a better artist. That is why nature provides such heartbreaking beauties: sunsets, storms, seas, mountains (Fuji to the Japanese, the Matterhorn to the Swiss). These heartbreaks are usually milder than those brought on by poetry or music, probably because nature is slower, less sudden, and less surprising. But hearts do leap suddenly into throats when an impossibly glorious vista suddenly appears around a corner or from behind a cloud.

This, too, is largely personal, but not wholly: everyone loves stars, seas, and sunsets, and no one gets misty-eyed over worms. (I foresee getting an angry letter from a worm lover and forestall it by admitting that there is indeed a glory even there. I draw the line between art and non-art only where God does, i.e., nowhere.) For me it is a great crashing wave of the sea that melts and glues my soul to it. (See my *The Sea Within*.) For many, it is a woman's face. (This is not an erotic but an aesthetic falling-in-love.) For Dante, it was Beatrice, whom he saw, not as an entity in the world like other entities, but as something like a hole in the world through which the light of Heaven shone. Dante's door in the world's walls was shaped like Beatrice. (See Charles Williams, *The Figure of Beatrice*, and Mary McDermott Shidler's *The Theology of Romantic Love*.) What was said of cathedrals above could be said of Beatrice, too, and vice versa. They are not merely things in this world but doors to another. They seem to the lover to be not natives to this world but otherworldly visitors.

The Iroquois called the quality such visitors emit *orenda*. They found it especially in rivers, oceans, stars, trees, and mountains. It is the spiritual sugar that lures us to places we cannot live in but only look at and love. The wonder and awe can also come from the discoveries of science, especially astronomy and astrophysics, as well as genetics and cell biology; from the astonishing and often literally unimaginable picture of the universe and the human body and brain that it reveals. Surely the most magnificent work of art of all is the universe itself: endlessly mysterious yet perfect in its order, even in its mathematical harmonies. As Edna St. Vincent Millay wrote: "Euclid alone has looked on beauty bare."[14]

God did not have to give us a cathedral to live in. He could have given us a Skinner box. Why did He create such a fantastic universe? For us, of course. We don't exist for gases and galaxies; they exist for us. We are the spiritual center, or point, of the universe. Copernicus was right only in a strictly material and quantitative sense. The older geo-centrism was more profoundly true spiritually. For God is our Father, and what Father makes babies for the sake of playpens rather than playpens for the sake of babies?

Some uneducated people in the past used to think the earth was flat rather than round. This was another premod-ern scientific mistake that is true spiritually, though it is not an edge you can fall off geographically. The real edge is death. Death is an absolute. Temporally, though not spa-tially, the world is flat, not round and relative. And death is the most obvious of all the doors in the walls of the world.

---

[14] Edna St. Vincent Millay, *Collected Poems* (New York: HarperCollins, 2011), 605.

In human nature, which is God's little universe in the big one, there is this big, obvious door called death. It is the worst thing in life and also the best; it is our "last enemy" (1 Cor 15:26) and also our only door to Heaven. Something like death, though not death itself as we now experience it, was in human nature from the beginning. Even if we had not fallen, we would not have remained in Eden forever; from the beginning we were caterpillars destined to fly as butterflies. The Fall did not change that; what it changed was the road, which was originally as easy as that of the caterpillar's but which became hard and narrow and rocky and dangerous and full of pain because of our sin and folly and rebellion and mistrust.

Unless death is abolished (probably by genetic engineering), there will always be at least one absolute in the world of relativities, one door in the walls of our Cave, one Jacob's Ladder to and from Heaven, one absolute edge to our world of time, if not of space. If and when death is abolished, I suspect that the Second Coming will follow very shortly, because "if those days had not been shortened, no human being would be saved" (Mt 24:22).

Perhaps this will be avoided. Perhaps mankind will suddenly acquire an honesty, a humility, a religious respect, a self-control, and a wisdom that it has never shown before in its entire lifetime concerning the use or non-use of a single new technological invention. If so, the next century or the next millennium may be the best ever. If not, it may well be the worst.

Based on our nature and our history, which scenario is more likely?

Have a nice day.

5. Christ as Divine Art

We are artists because our Father is an artist. We are creators because we are created in the image of our Creator. God's art is better than ours. But God's art is not first of all nature but Christ.

Christ's divine nature is not art, because it is not made; it is eternal. But Christ's human nature is made in time: a joint effort of His Father and His mother. It is the greatest of all works of art. It is also the greatest door.

Christ said, "I am the door" (Jn 10:9). All the doors we have explored are parts of this door, as all words are parts of the Word. All the doors are Christ in disguise.

When we use any door, we are dealing with Christ. For all doors are like Jacob's Ladder, and Christ clearly identified Himself as Jacob's Ladder. (Compare Genesis 28:12 with John 1:51.)

This is true of both supernatural doors and natural doors. Because of Christ, there are other supernatural doors: miracles, grace, conversions, visions, special providences, visitors from Heaven (and Hell), the Jews in history, prophets, saints, the Eucharist. But even the natural doors we have been exploring, such as the inherent providential plot of our story, and human arts like music, are about the divine Logos, the Mind of God.

There are many other natural doors.

Children are doors. Children are like Transubstantiation: a divine miracle in which something eternal newly enters time.

Existence is a door, for no assemblage of essences or natures accounts for it. As Wittgenstein says, "It is not *how* the world is but *that* it is, that is mystical."[15]

[15] Ludwig Wittgenstein, *Tractatus Logico-Philosophicus* 6.44.

The question Heidegger called "the fundamental question of metaphysics", namely, "Why are there beings at all instead of nothing?",[16] is such a door. Your unique individuality is such a door, for no assemblage of attributes makes it up. If you had an absolutely identical twin, you would be just as absolutely individual, unique, and irreplaceable as you are now. The intrinsic value of each individual human being is such a door, for nothing else in the universe has intrinsic value, only relative value.

Through all the doors we meet Christ the Mind (Logos) of God the Creator. All doors are the Door in disguise (Jn 10:9).

For Christ is cosmic. All other ancient deities are local, but Christ is cosmic. As Teilhard de Chardin says in *The Divine Milieu*,

At the heart of our universe, each soul exists for God, in our Lord.

But all reality, even material reality, around each one of us, exists for our souls. Hence, all sensible reality, around each one of us, exists, through our souls, for God in our Lord . . . .[17]

As our humanity assimilates the material world, and as the Host assimilates our humanity, the Eucharistic transformation goes beyond and completes the transubstantiation of the bread on the altar. Step by step it irresistibly invades the universe. It is the fire that sweeps over the heath; the stroke that vibrates through the bronze. In a secondary and generalised sense, but in a true sense, the sacramental Species are formed by the totality of the world, and the duration of the creation is the time needed for its consecration. In

[16] Martin Heidegger, *Introduction to Metaphysics*, trans. Gregory Fried and Richard Polt. 2nd ed. (New Haven, Conn.: Yale Univ. Press, 2014), 1.

[17] Teilhard de Chardin, *The Divine Milieu* (New York: Harper Perennial Classics, 2001), 19.

Christ vivimus, movemur et sumus [we live and move and have our being].[18]

Our work appears to us, in the main, as a way of earning our daily bread. But its essential virtue is on a higher level: through it we complete in ourselves the subject of the divine union. . . . Hence, whatever our role as men may be, whether we are artists, working men, or scholars, we can, if we are Christians, speed towards the object of our work as though towards an opening [a door!] on to the supreme fulfilment of our beings. . . .

We ought to accustom ourselves to this basic truth till we are steeped in it, until it becomes as familiar to us as the perception of shape or the reading of words. God . . . is not far away from us, altogether apart from the world we see, touch, hear, smell and taste about us. Rather he awaits us every instant in our action, in the work of the moment. . . . He is at the tip of my pen, my spade, my brush, my needle.[19]

[18] Ibid., 98.
[19] Ibid., 27–28.

Conclusions

I originally intended to write two more chapters. One was on how to apply this vision to your life. If you are an agnostic, you can still apply 90 percent of the sentences in this book; if you are a non-Christian theist, 95 percent; if you are a Protestant Christian, 99 percent, and if you are a Catholic, 100 percent. I decided instead to let you write that chapter with your life.

The other chapter was going to be a refutation of reductionism, the opposite philosophy of life from the one in this book. (See the beginning of chapter 1.) But that last chapter would have changed the tone, though not the message, of the book from something positive to something negative and from something intuitive to something argumentative. It would have made the ending of the book long and sour, so I will try to make my refutation of reductionism short and sweet instead.

Suffice it to say that all reductionisms, like all skepticisms, are logically self-contradictory. Skepticism is self-contradictory whatever form it takes: Is it true that there is no truth? Certain that nothing is certain? Absolutely no absolutes? A universal truth that there are no universal truths? Dogmatically given that there are no dogmas given? An objective truth that truth is not objective? Sociologically or psychologically relative that everything is sociologically or psychologically relative? A myth that all is a myth? Guaranteed by God that there is no God? An illusion that all is illusion? The game takes many forms, but you can never win it.

Similarly with reductionism. If love is only lust, thought only cerebral biochemistry, reasoning only rationalization, gods only myths, justice only power, choice only unperceived necessity, eternity only time's dream, etcetera, the formula for that "nothing buttery" is that A is nothing but B, that A is only B—but that means that there is *in all reality* no A, or dimension of A, that is more than B. But you can know that only if you know all reality or all dimensions of reality. And for that, you must have total, all-encompassing intelligence; in other words, you must be God.

If you do not think you are God, then welcome to the ranks of at least the open-minded agnostics, those who are not sure that there is no door in the wall, that no angel will ever greet you, etc. If you do think you are God, I thank you for not punishing me for disbelieving in you.

You cannot justify by the scientific method the principle that everything can be reduced to the scientific method. And since that scientific reductionism is a choice, not a logical necessity, and not only a choice but a logically self-contradictory choice, what in the world is motivating you to make that choice and to live it? Why do you *want* to deny human dignity, freedom, and spirituality? You don't have to. Why do you want to chop off your head?

That's the sort of thing I was going to say in the last chapter. But I decided not to, because it's much too negative, downbeat, carping, critical, rationalistic, abstract, and personally insulting. I'd much rather end with Beethoven and with Sam's tears.

Wouldn't you?

APPENDIX I

Recommendations for
Further Explorations

Plato, especially *Gorgias*; *Republic*, books 6, 7, and 10; and
Phaedo

Plotinus, especially the *Ennead* "On Beauty"

Augustine, especially his *Confessions*

John of the Cross (begin with Father Thomas Dubay's *The
Fire Within*)

Pascal's *Pensées*

Kierkegaard (begin with Robert Bretall's *A Kierkegaard An-
thology*)

G. K. Chesterton, especially *Orthodoxy*, *The Everlasting Man*,
and *The Man Who Was Thursday*

George MacDonald, *The Golden Key*

H. G. Wells, "The Door in the Wall"

J. R. R. Tolkien, *The Lord of the Rings*, *The Silmarillion*, and
"On Fairy-Stories"

C. S. Lewis, *Surprised by Joy*, *Miracles*, *Letters to Malcolm*, *Pere-
landra*, *Till We Have Faces*, and "The Weight of Glory"

Peter Kreeft, *Heaven, the Heart's Deepest Longing*

APPENDIX II

When Is It "Enough"?

"More" has two opposites, "Less" and "Enough". "Less" is reductionism, the philosophy of both modernism and post-modernism. (See the introduction on the three philosophies of life.) I have said enough about that. But I think I should also say something about Enough. What is its proper place? Here is my answer:

"Enough"

It was not enough
Being only One;
Thus His timeless act:
Fathering the Son.

It was not enough
Timeless Two to be;
Overflow of love
Makes Them timeless Three.

It was not enough
Being God alone;
Angel minds He made
To know and be known.

It was not enough
Making only spirit;
He made matter's music
And the ears to hear it.

It was not enough
Making minds and atoms;
Fusing them together,
He made sirs and madams.

It was not enough
Giving them a garden;
They invented sin,
He invented pardon.

It was not enough
Pardoning the sinning;
God received a mother,
God got a beginning.

It was not enough
In their flesh to dwell;
To save their place in Heaven
He took their place in Hell.

It was not enough
Sun and moon were shaken;
See upon the Cross
God by God forsaken.

It was not enough
Raising up the dead;
To feed our starving souls
He became our Bread.

It was not enough
That He share His house;
He would share His bed,
Make each soul His spouse.

When is it enough?
Ask the mighty River
Flowing on forever
With Love's holy water.
Hear the answer: "Never!"

Peter Kreeft,
from *An Ocean Full of Angels*